BODY TALK

BODY TALK

THE SKILLS OF POSITIVE IMAGE

JUDI JAMES

THE INDUSTRIAL SOCIETY

First published in 1995 by
The Industrial Society
Robert Hyde House
48 Bryanston Square
London W1H 7LN
Telephone: 0171–262–2401

© Judi James 1995
Typographical arrangement © The Industrial Society 1995

ISBN 1 85835 153 7

British Library Cataloguing-in-Publication Data.
A catalogue record for this book is available from the
British Library

Typeset by: The Midlands Book Typesetting Company Loughborough
Printed by: Lavenham Press
Cover design: Nicky Downes
Cartoons: Martin Shovel
Illustrations: Chris Le Cluse

The Industrial Society is a Registered Charity No. 290003

CONTENTS

introduction

We have no idea how we look to other people — and for most of us ignorance is bliss. A quick glance in the mirror in the morning is enough to check the tie is straight and the hair's in place and then — give or take the odd preen or two during the day — we're happy for the rest of the world to take us pretty much as it finds us.

The trouble is, that reflection tells lies — and that person we see staring back at us from the mirror has very little to do with the way others perceive us. When we study our own image we play a game of self-deception, seeing what we *want* to see, rather than what really exists.

Looking in the mirror makes it very difficult to catch ourselves unawares. We pose when we stand in front of it and we pull faces that we don't use in everyday life.

We've seen ourselves too often to be objective about the visual messages we're sending out — things that *we* find important in our appearance can go unnoticed by other people, while things we rarely see, like our own facial expressions and body language, will be busy relaying vital signals that we never stop to assess.

Occasionally — perhaps with an important interview or meeting looming — we might invest in a little more navel-contemplation than usual. This is when well-meaning friends will start churning out totally unproductive platitudes like:

'JUST BE YOURSELF'

Fine. Easy-peasy. So what is the *real* you actually like? Suited and booted at all times, with a ready smile and a confident turn of phrase? Most of us are slobs deep down — is that the sort of image you think would be suitable for the important occasion? Is honesty always the best policy for interviews and business meetings?

When the chips are down many of us lack confidence in ourselves and our abilities. Surely it would be better to mask some of that diffidence and at least give the appearance of knowing what we're talking about?

'LET PEOPLE TAKE YOU AS THEY FIND YOU'

Fine again. So if you don't get the job you're after because you were inappropriately dressed it's the interviewer's problem — right? This marketing method goes hand-in-hand with the 'I always speak my mind' school of thought. When people warn you that they always speak their minds they often believe it gives them carte blanche to be opinionated and impolite.

Life is full of compromise. When we speak to people we vary our choice of words and tone to be agreeable and clearly understood. We should do the same with our visual communications, too.

'YOU'LL NEVER PLEASE EVERYONE'

True — but it's no reason not to try. Everyone has his or her own idea of what looks right. We all have our own tastes and we all have our own opinions. This is why most businessmen dress in the 'uniform' of a navy or grey suit. Because they all look the same there is no fear of 'saying' the wrong thing. By displaying similar tastes to their male colleagues and clients they avoid inviting any initial prejudice.

We like people who look like us. We believe it means they think like us, too. The advantages of this system usually outweigh those nasty moments when words like 'boring', 'bland' and 'cloning' rear their ugly little heads.

MIRACLES

This book is not a 'quick-fix' guide and it is not full of speedy miracles. Buying a bright red jacket or tie will not guarantee you instant success and neither will changing your hair parting or wearing a spanking new fuchsia lipstick.

External make-overs are only effective if the internal image is positive, too. Hang a loud tie round the neck of a boring person and he will only look like a boring person in

a loud tie. Getting a new haircut when your confidence is
at a low ebb will only make you look as ghastly as you
already feel.

SO WHAT IS IMAGE AND WHAT CAN IT DO FOR ME?

Your image could be described as the depiction of yourself
that you show to the rest of the world.

An effective image should be one that works *for*, rather
than against, you. It is a true reflection of your better
qualities and should be genuine and sincere, not slick or
phoney or over-rehearsed.

You can use your image to throw a smoke-screen around
your faults and deficiencies — but there is a limit to how
long you can keep that smoke-screen up and how effective
it will be.

Image is useful as a marketing tool — but you can only
market a product you have belief in — which is why this
book will place as much emphasis on the internal as the
external image.

1 positive marketing – assessing the product

'The will to win is nothing unless you have the will to prepare' — Anon.

If you look at image as a marketing technique then you have to become acquainted with the product you intend to market.

The three key steps for positive marketing are simple and easy to plan:

1. know your objectives

What do you want and where do you want to get to? Are you ambitious? What is important in your life? How would you like other people to perceive you?

> INSTANT PLANNING EXERCISE:
>
> *Sit down with a large piece of paper and set out your short and long-term goals, both in business and home life.*
> *Work out how many of those goals are realistic and achievable and how many are just idealistic dreams. Don't dismiss any of the 'dreams' too easily, though. Think about the possibilities rather than the probabilities before you reject them.*

> *Remember — anything can be possible if you try — if*
> *you don't try, nothing happens. Keep an open mind.*
>
> *Playing with Goals*
> *Take one of the life's goals that you dismissed as*
> *'fantasy' or 'unrealistic'. Use it as an exercise to see*
> *what may be achieved if you try. The more fantastic*
> *the idea the more useful the exercise.*
> *Let's suppose you said you wanted to be a rock star or*
> *a multi-millionaire. Take a blank sheet of paper and*
> *write that as your goal across the top.*
> *Now list one column of 'assets' you already have to help*
> *you to achieve that dream, and one of 'drawbacks'.*
> *Then formulate a businesslike plan to eliminate those*
> *drawbacks and achieve your goal.*

Dismiss nothing at first — even the most ridiculous ideas. Brainstorm, writing down all possibilities and only crossing out the unlikely ones after a lot of thought. Try some research — how do people become millionaires, for instance? What careers do they tend to be in? What steps did they take to get there? Once you have run through the techniques for this scenario you can apply them to some of your more achievable goals.

Many leading businesspeople make written lists of the things they want to achieve on a daily basis, before they start work. Setting goals like this makes us more successful by making us more action-centred.

If you have no idea where you're going then the only place you're sure to end up is nowhere. Once you've decided on your destination, though, all you need to do next is plan your route.

2. know your product

Understand yourself. Know your strengths as well as your weaknesses. Be aware of your achievements and positive abilities.

MOTIVATIONS:

Start with a little voyage of self-discovery. Answer this handful of basic questions:

1. Choose six words you feel would best describe your personality in business.
2. And six words you feel a work colleague would use to describe you.
3. Another six words you think a close friend outside work would use.
4. What were your ambitions as a child?
5. What ambitions do you have now?
6. Name three principles you would consider worth fighting for.
7. Name the three people you admire most.
8. What gives you the most satisfaction in your career?
9. What would you most like to do for a living?
10. What makes you angry?
11. What makes you happy?

Study the list. Were you surprised by any of the answers? When we were children we were quite unashamed of our own dreams and goals and emotions but as we grow older we lose touch with all three — often getting too bogged-down by day-to-day problems and goals to contemplate the more long-term ones.

We can even lose sight of what makes us happy — yet both ambitions and happiness need to be worked at before they can be achieved. Work requires planning. With the correct planning anything is possible.

CONFIDENCE

We all need to nurture an inner confidence in ourselves before we can start work on the external image. If we lack that confidence in our abilities we will need to be extremely determined liars, because we will be marketing a product we have no faith in.

Being confident about our abilities is not being immodest. No one's expecting you to go around shouting all your good points from the rooftops, but knowing what you're good at makes marketing those qualities a whole lot less difficult.

3. learn how to market that product

Once you understand yourself and your goals you will find it easier to start effective marketing. Without a list of objectives, though, you will be marketing nothing special to no one in particular.

Some people are better at marketing themselves than others. Did you ever work with someone who always seemed to be in the right place at the right time doing the right thing when the manager was around? That's called effective self-marketing.

Did you ever find hard work going unnoticed but then get caught having a quick yawn and asked if you'd been sleeping all day? Or did you ever notice that no one sees when you're early for work but everyone notices when you turn up late? That's bad personal marketing.

Maybe you think good marketing is just down to good luck. It isn't. It's a skill — and like any other skill, it can be learnt.

FIRST IMPRESSIONS

'It's better to be looked over than overlooked' — Mae West.

It can take as little as four seconds to create a first impression and four years to 'uncreate' it if it happens to be unfavourable.

A first impression is based on false assumptions and prejudice but, because it is essentially a subconscious process — with most of us drawing speedy conclusions about one another without once ever stopping to fathom out why — there is very little we can do to stop it taking place.

Did you ever meet anyone you disliked on sight? Did you

7

take time to work out why, or did you just put it down to intuition?

We live in a busy world and — if you live in a city — you will encounter hundreds of people a day. We simply don't have time to sit down and get to know each one properly, so we allow our eyes to handle the first stages of the sifting-out process.

Within the first few seconds of meeting someone our subconscious has quite cheerfully made several assumptions about his or her status and personality. The fact that most of those assumptions will be wrong rarely troubles us. We like to think we have 'got the measure' of people as soon as possible.

What makes this first impression even more dangerous is that it can easily become a self-fulfilling prophecy. If we don't like the look of someone new at first sight, then it is very tempting to act negatively towards him or her. When they see us behaving like that they will often respond in kind. This will delight us because it confirms our initial impression and we will go away happy that we can always 'spot the bad ones'.

Whether first impressions are accurate or not, though, the important fact to remember is that we should be aware of the impression we make on first meeting. How do we come across? What types of signals do we send out? What are our own silent communications like? What is it we are saying to other people before we even open our mouths? The best way to discover this is by analysing exactly how we judge other people.

It is easy to worry too much about *what* we say to people, rather than *how* we said it. Albert Mehrabian did some research to discover exactly what it is that contributes to the total message and the results are astonishing:

> Verbal — 7%
> Tone of Voice — 38%
> Visual — 55%

Words take a definite back seat when compared to the impact of vocal tone and the non-verbal images. If you say one thing and your body language gives out a contradictory message, it is the visual image that will be perceived as the truth — and the one that will be remembered longer.

VISUAL IMPACT

So how is a First Impression created? If we analyse our own subconscious thoughts we can discover how we are making instant assumptions about people — and then we can turn that analysis back on ourselves. The main areas of visual impact are:

1. FACIAL EXPRESSION — Eye contact, the smile or the frown are all powerful messages of visual communication.
2. BODY LANGUAGE — We need to understand what our posture and gestures tell others about us.
3. DRESS — When we choose the clothes we are going to

wear each day we display things like taste, personality and attitude to the rest of the world. If we dress like others in a group we show what 'club' we belong to. If we decide to dress differently we tell people we like to be viewed as an outsider or loner or even eccentric.

4.   GROOMING — Hair, hands, and smell will all go to form an important part of the total image we create.

You can see from this list how hard it is to judge your own visual communications. When did you last see your own facial expressions? Or your own body language? Maybe when you looked in the mirror — but then we've already established that the mirror tells lies.

So we are constantly employing a major communication skill without knowing what it is we are saying to other people. Does that sound dangerous? It should!

One of the aims of this book is to help you to take control of those visual messages, just as you control the words that come out of your month — by planning, analysing and, most important of all, knowing what it is you want to say in the first place.

POSITIVE CHANGE

'The only thing we have to fear is fear itself'
— Franklin Roosevelt.

People don't like change. It makes them feel uncomfortable and fearful. Sometimes they will put up with quite dreadful circumstances because they fear the alternative might be worse. Still more wonderful adages have been spun over the years to put the wind up us when we consider trying something new:

'Better the devil you know than the devil you don't.'
'Out of the frying pan into the fire.'
'A bird in the hand is worth two in the bush.'
'If it ain't broke, don't fix it.'

Of course, you might also consider that improvements only come about as a result of change. Being receptive to change is vital if you mean to spring-clean your image. And it's no good just dipping your toe in the water. Some people will try changes for a short period of time just to prove to themselves they were doing it right in the first place. They don't give the changes a chance.

There are a lot of positive aspects to change, though:

1.   It can lead to improvement
2.   It can prevent us getting bored.
3.   It can build self-respect and confidence.
4.   It can stop other people taking us for granted.

TASTES

Our tastes and belief in our abilities become programmed very early on in life. At school we are quickly filtered into certain subjects we are considered good at so that we can pass exams in them — discarding others that we may have enjoyed in the process.

We then begin to believe that we are good at some things and hopeless at others. We tend to avoid the subjects we were told we had failed at and spend the rest of our lives keeping up this charade, telling ourselves and others:

'I'm no good with figures — I'm useless at maths.'
or: 'I was always hopeless with my hands — I can't draw or paint to save my life.'

What we mean is we gave up without really trying.

We start to have set likes and dislikes for things like food and music for no particular reason and we begin to see certain clothes as being either 'us' or 'not us'.

These early decisions may handicap us throughout our lives. We will consider ourselves to lack certain skills for no real reason. When people say they aren't good at things like car mechanics, cooking, setting the video or speaking in public it usually means they have decided that themselves, without an open-minded attempt. Some early programming may have made them lack the confidence to try their best when they are older.

Many things are an acquired taste. If you allow yourself to be put off the first time you could be missing a lot.

Remember: keep an open mind.
Try it — you might like it!
Be receptive and positive to change and new things.
Be positive about your own skills and prepared to develop others.

twelve-point positive action plan

Try taking as many of these steps as you can over the next week to improve your attitude and well-being:

1. Read a light-hearted novel or go to see a funny film.
2. Treat yourself to something that is cheap but fun and daring and wear it — a loud tie, coloured socks, green nailvarnish etc.
3. Pamper your body with a healthy diet — low fat cooking, fresh fruits and vegetables, high carbohydrate and fibre.
4. Watch cheerful tv programmes and avoid all gloomy news in the newspapers. Push any worries into next week.
5. Buy flowers for your desk at work.
6. Spend an hour doing something silly you've never done before — baking a cake, clay modelling, playing snap, watching a cartoon on video.
7. Compliment other people — at least three a day.
8. Avoid other moaners — no matter how bad their problems make your excuses and leave. This is your week off!
9. Get brochures and plan an exotic holiday — dreaming costs nothing!
10. Get some exercise each day — even if it's just a long walk.
11. Avoid caffeine and alcohol.
12. Telephone an old friend you've lost touch with.

2 confidence and a positive viewpoint

Ask most people what quality they would like to have more of and they usually say 'confidence'. We all feel handicapped by nerves or shyness at some time in our lives and — when we do — we assume everyone else around us is overflowing with confidence and self-possession. We are the only ones attacked by self-doubt and we are the only ones suffering.

Of course this isn't true, but merely the way we perceive the situation — just as someone speaking in public will be led by nerves to believe the audience is against the speaker or laughing at him or her, and someone attending an interview will assume all the other candidates must be much better qualified for the job.

When we lack confidence we question everything. We think too long before we speak and we start to doubt our own abilities. Even if we're sure about our skills we can have trouble selling ourselves on occasions like interviews or meetings.

so how can I build my confidence?

The best way is by being objective about yourself. Drop all the worries and inhibitions you're carrying around like surplus baggage and take a look at yourself from the opposite side of the desk.

What exactly are your good points? Analyse them like a marketing expert studying a new client. Don't bother being modest because this assessment is just between you and yourself.

Imagine you were interviewing yourself for a job. What would you think of this person on first meeting? What would you consider his or her positive qualities? What's so good about the person and what might make you like him or her?

POSITIVE ACTION EXERCISE

Take a large blank sheet of paper and start to draw a brick wall, building up a row at a time.
Fill the bottom row with bricks that describe your academic achievements — all the exam passes and

courses taken. This row should be easy to compile — it's the sorts of things you would like on a CV.
Build up the next row with skills you have that you may not have passed exams in. Don't be negative — nothing is too small to be listed. Can you use a computer? Swim? Cook? Paint a picture? Ski? Don't qualify it by adding, 'Yes, but not very well.' Write it down anyway.
Fill the next row with achievements — and these should be achievements by your own standards, not anyone else's. Perhaps you did some work for charity. Maybe you have a fear of water but swam a dozen strokes in the pool on holiday. Did you organize something at work or apply for a promotion when your fears were telling you not to bother?
The last row should be filled with personal pluses — positive points about your personality. Are you reliable? Cheerful? Honest? Flexible? Make your own positive assessments and list the results.
When your wall is finished study the results. These are the things about you that you should be marketing. They are the reasons why people like you and why you are good at your job. They are also the reasons why you like yourself.
Add to the wall if you think of more points. As you build it up you should be building your inner confidence — knowing what it is you are good at and where your strengths lie. Now you are aware of your strengths it's time to work on your feelings.

creating confidence

Confidence is not a skill that can be acquired overnight, it is something to build slowly, step by step. No matter how small the steps seem at times, always make sure they're going in the right direction.

Confidence is not a constant, either. You may lack it generally or you may find certain situations or people make you react in a less assertive way. Given time and encouragement we can all do a job well enough, but these two qualities are always a luxury in modern business life. People are competitive, too. If you act unsure you will find people treading over you, rather than stopping to help.

To work on your inner confidence you need to try the following steps. These may mean changing the habits of a lifetime, but, as we have already established, change is necessary if we are to go forward.

1. STOP CRITICIZING YOURSELF

Self criticism is boring to listen to, and it's destructive, rather than constructive. We do it as a defence mechanism — if we cast the first stone then maybe others will be more tolerant of our faults. This is obviously rubbish. Be nice about yourself. When we constantly pick out our shortcomings, even jokingly, we bring them to the attention of others. Shut up. Maybe they haven't even noticed.

Can you take a compliment? What if you were told some work you'd done was good. Which response would you choose?

'Oh, it wasn't that difficult really, it didn't take long.'
'Yes, I did it, but I'm sure I've made a mess of it.'
'Oh, you're just saying that.'
'Anyone could have done it better.'

Or, quite simply:

'Thank you.'

2. STOP MOANING

Whingeing doesn't make problems vanish — instead it can just be a negative way of dealing with them. And it's boring to listen to.

Tackle things in a businesslike, active manner — that way you'll have more self-respect as well as more respect from your colleagues. Plan the way in which you deal with things. Does the problem have a solution? If so, what is the best way of achieving it? Either put up or shut up. Give

is the winning formula. This is the role you will be acting out the next time you have to deal with this situation.

Concentrate on this newer, more positive you — and step into this person's shoes, rather than the first, more negative person's before you approach the scene in real life. See it working, see yourself doing well and use that image as your self-fulfilling prophecy, rather than the first one.

action plan

Now you're working with more positive thoughts it's time to start finding out even more about yourself. In the first chapter we worked on some of the basic self-discovery questions. Now it's time to discover more about the business side of your life.

Take a pen and paper and ask yourself the following questions. Brainstorm the replies — don't get writer's block, just throw down the first answers that occur to you — you can always go back and change them later on.

1. How would you *like* others at work to perceive you? Is this a constant? Or would you make two lists — 'How I would like my colleagues to see me' and 'How I would like my boss to see me'. Study the differences.

2. Are there any talents or skills you have that are not being used in your present job? Does this make you resentful or frustrated? Do you have an outlet for these skills in your personal life? Could you find one?

3. Do you prefer working in a team or by yourself?

4. Name the last time you did something at work you were proud of. Did you reward yourself at the time or did you look for reward or thanks from others?

5. Think hard and be honest — which of these gives you the most satisfaction in your job?

   Praise from customers

   Praise from the boss

Public displays of gratitude — e.g. awards nights, etc
Self-praise — knowing you have done the job well
Money — your income or bonuses
Fame
Complaining to everyone that no one values you
enough
Companionship — mixing with colleagues — social
events, etc

6. Name something that has worried you in business
   recently.
7. If you were invited to a reunion from an old job out of
   the blue would you be excited by the prospect or
   worry that you were too fat/wrinkled/unsuccessful/
   boring to enjoy seeing old friends?
8. If the boss asked to see you in his or her office would
   you expect a pay rise or assume you had done
   something wrong?
9. If someone pays you a compliment do you thank them
   or start proving them wrong, e.g.: *'This jacket? Oh, it
   was only cheap and I've had it for years.'*
10. Do you feel people with less ability than you get on
    better through luck?
11. What do you feel most prevents you getting what you
    want in your career?
12. Imagine that 'something' had vanished overnight.
    Describe in detail exactly how your life would change.

There are no right or wrong answers to these questions,
just treat them as a means of self-discovery.

Read your answers through and try to get an objective
view of the person who wrote them. Is there anything
wrong with your answers? Do you sound like a positive,
confident person, or a negative, diffident one? Is how you
are the same as how you would like to be? If not, are you
prepared to change?

Start considering an action plan to implement those
changes. Set yourself a time target — plan to do the quiz
again in a few weeks or a few months and see if the
answers differ.

3 individuality

During the exercises in Chapters One and Two you will have discovered a few extra facts. Firstly — that you still have negative qualities along with the positive ones. Well, that's OK — nobody said we were building a perfect human being and we are who we are because of our weaknesses as well as our strengths.

Nobody is good at everything, just as nobody is bad at everything, either.

Secondly — you will have seen that very few of your personality qualities are constant. Well, that's OK, too — different circumstances make us react in different ways. We adapt and change according to our surroundings and who we are dealing with — that's how we survive. Extroverts can be shy in certain types of company and the most aggressive person will act passively under certain conditions.

What we have to do is to get a sense of perspective and see our worst points set in relation to the best. What we have to avoid doing is becoming programmed into a negative response to events, saying things like:

'I'm *always* so clumsy.'
'I'm *never* lucky at games.'
'I'm *always* in the wrong queue.'
'People *always* take me for granted.'
'I'm *always* late — I can never get anywhere on time.'
'I *always* get nervous at interviews.'
'No one *ever* laughs at my jokes.'
'The traffic lights are *always* on red when I'm in a hurry.'
'It *always* rains when I have my hair done.'
'I could *never* get up and give a talk in public.'

This is pessimism (and possibly paranoia) at its most destructive worst. If you look at life in this way and expect the worst then it will probably come true. Try spotting and commenting on the good things that happen to you, instead.

happiness

Did you ever notice how, when you're happy, the whole world seems to look better? Nothing has changed, though, apart from your angle of perception.

What exactly makes you happy? Money? A full social life? A rewarding, well-paid job? Did you ever wonder why pools-winners claimed the money had no positive effect on their lives, and think you would be happy if you had a large windfall?

Psychologists have studied the 'happiness factor' for years and the results are surprising. One theory is that good things in our lives increase our happiness level a little less each time they happen.

American psychologist Harry Helson claims our happiness has an 'adaptation level'. If life fails to live up to our expectations we are unhappy as a result. If what we expect to happen happens we are neither happy nor unhappy. If what happens *surpasses* our expectations, however, we're usually happy. But the more good things that happen, the higher our level of expectation becomes, making it harder for us to be happy.

It is our view of life and its events that makes us happy or unhappy, rather than the events themselves. The optimist will always see the glass as half-full, while to the pessimist it is half-empty.

NEGATIVE SPEECH

Look for the optimistic viewpoint, even if you are sceptical at first. Tell people about your likes, rather than your dislikes. Sound keen, rather than cynical. If you can't think of anything positive to say then say nothing. Avoid the use of negative words and phrases, like:

Can't

Won't

But — as in: *'that sounds OK, but . . .'*

Shouldn't

Impossible

Never

Avoid other whingers, too. Moaning is very contagious — however good your mood it's difficult to sustain it after prolonged ear-bashing from someone who enjoys being negative about everything.

OWN GOALS

Set your own standards for personal success, instead of comparing your own achievements to those of others. If you're a good driver by your own estimation then you're a good driver — you don't have to compare yourself to Damon Hill or Nigel Mansell.

It is far easier to be jealous or envious of someone else's skill or luck than it is to go out and work on those achievements yourself. Then — if we do try — we take any failure as confirmation of the fact that we should never have bothered in the first place. If we succeed, we immediately set about running down our own successes by being inappropriately modest. Therefore we end up in a no-win situation.

Remember: One failure doesn't make *you* a failure.
Forgive yourself when you screw up.

And: Praise yourself when you do succeed, however small the successes. Value your achievements and treat yourself with rewards or self-praise.

VALUES

Take control of your own values. Self-assessment is a valuable tool if it is realistic. Often we assess ourselves through the eyes of others, without knowing what those people think.

Listen to other opinions and criticisms but don't invent them. When we lack confidence it is all too easy to second-guess a negative reaction from other people.

If you are nervous before speaking to a group, for example, your mind will go into a spiral of anxiety of its own making. Negative thoughts fight their way to the surface and you start asking yourself questions like these:

'What if they don't like me?'
'What if I make a fool of myself?'
'What if I run out of things to say?'
'What if they ask questions and I don't know the answers?'

The more nervous you get, the more such questions become unshakeable fact:

'I *know* they won't like me.'
'I *know* I will make a fool of myself.'
'I *know* I will run out of things to say.'
'I *know* they're going to ask me difficult questions that I can't answer.'

By the time you get up to speak you are primed to make these nightmares reality. Then you can be smugly sure that your judgement was sound:

'I *knew* I was going to make a hash of it — I'm no good at speaking in public. I'll never try again.'

It feels good when you're right, doesn't it?

TAKING CONTROL

So — just who is making the decisions in your life? You dress in a certain way, eat certain foods, have hobbies and tastes in music and art. You go out socially, you read a certain newspaper and you drive a certain type of car.

How many of those things do you and you alone decide upon? Or how much are you influenced by the opinions of others — real or imagined?

Pretend you have gone into a shop to buy a coat. Hanging on the rack is the sort of coat you know you should get — sensible colour, classic cut, quality fabric. Hanging next to it, though, is a coat you really like —

bright yellow, way-out style, fashionable fabric. When you try it on it looks good on you, so why not have it? Are you using sound logic to make the decision, or faulty logic?

Good Logic
- It's too expensive.
- The colour doesn't flatter me.
- The fabric is poor quality — it wouldn't last.
- It's not appropriate for my job or the company I work for.
- It would get dirty too quickly.

Faulty Logic
- I wouldn't be out shopping in the first place — my partner chooses my clothes for me. (So did your mother when you were a kid — grow up and make your own decisions.)
- It's not really 'me' (If you like it, it *is*.)
- I would never dare to wear it. (Cowardice.)
- People would think I looked stupid. (They might think you look good — maybe they've been thinking you looked stupid for years in that old plain navy mac you've been wearing.)
- My partner wouldn't like it. (*You* are the one who is going to wear it.)
- My kids would take the mickey. (They will whatever you wear. Kids are like that. Have you ever looked at some of the clothes they buy?)

This form of faulty logic will affect us if we try to improve our business image by looking smarter and more professional. What will our colleagues think? Will they make sarcastic remarks? Will they think we're after a pay rise or promotion?

So what if they do? So what if you are?

In a comfortable rut
Friends, family and colleagues like us to stay the way we are– that way, they feel comfortable with us because they know what to expect.

Colleagues may even feel threatened by any upgrading of our image — if we improve it may make them look worse. Laughter and sarcasm will be their way of getting us back to the way we were.

It's up to you to decide whether you are doing things for them or for yourself. Who do you most want to please? Who do you want in control of your life? Who should be making the decisions?

FLEXIBILITY

Once you have decided to take responsibility for your own actions, though, there is still scope for flexibility when you are dealing with others. Being more confident doesn't mean being yourself at all times, come what may. Different people need different handling and we all have to be tolerant and sympathetic to the needs of others.

Everyone has his or her own set of behavioural styles and patterns and (although there should be no need to change that style) it is sometimes advisable to moderate it.

Psychologists have simplified these behavioural styles into four main categories:

The Entertainer Talkative and lively with a good sense of humour, these people can seem like the life and soul of the party. They like meeting people and getting on with them and prefer face-to-face meetings to talks over the telephone.

The Bully Assertive, sometimes to the point of being aggressive, these people like things done their own way, and so like to be leaders. Impatient and speedy, they will not tolerate fools gladly.

The Nice Guy Pleasant and easygoing, these people like to be liked. They will be supportive and thoughtful and hate upsetting anybody.

The Facts and Figures Person Quiet, deliberate, slow to make decisions and then only after hearing all points of view, these people like working with figures and statistics and will often work better alone. They don't like waffle, they like to be presented with solid facts. They are not people who use humour a lot.

You can see how each of these 'types' could be successful in business, but also how they would have trouble getting along with one another if they didn't modify their styles and behaviour patterns. There's nothing wrong with doing this and it doesn't mean you are losing your individuality. All it means is that you are getting along with other people by respecting the fact that they may have different styles from your own.

4 a working image

There are three main reasons why image is so important in the workplace:

1. The Feel-Good Factor
2. Corporate Image
3. Self Marketing

1. the feel-good factor

If you look good you feel good, or, if you *think* you look good you feel good. Sometimes the two things are not the same — remember we have already established we don't know what we look like to other people.

Feeling confident about your image will make you feel more confident about yourself. The reverse, then, is also true. Ever have a lousy haircut at the hairdresser or barber? Remember how your confidence dipped to an all-time low as you walked about with it sitting on your head? Remember how no matter how many people told you it suited you or looked good, you still felt as bad? That's because your own perceived image had taken a body-blow. You *felt* you looked lousy and it didn't matter what anyone else thought.

On the other hand we all have clothes that make us feel fit to take on the world — something we would choose to wear to an interview or a tricky business meeting. A tie that we feel good in or a jacket that gives us that extra oomph. Putting it on is like putting on armour. That is the feel-good factor. It's important — never underestimate it.

Confidence is all in the mind. If that tie or that jacket helps — use it.

FORWARD PLANNING

This is why it's important to set aside some time to plan
your outfit for the next day. Business dress is a decision
better taken the night before than first thing in the
morning, when you're in a hurry. Plan to use clothes that
you feel good in; check that they're all matching and in
good condition for wearing.

Laddered tights, odd socks, stained ties and creased
shirts make us look and feel bewildered and lazy. It's a bad
way to start the day. Be kind to yourself — arrange things
in advance.

Treat yourself occasionally to something that will give
you a bit of a boost — this needn't be a whole new outfit,
but anything new that makes you feel a bit different. A new
tie — a different lipstick — a tiepin when you don't
normally wear one — snazzy braces for a change, instead
of a belt — an unusual brooch — these things can be a
cheap way to stop you feeling your image is in a rut.

2. corporate image

Whether we like it or not we are responsible for creating
the image of the company we work for. Very few companies

realize this, though. Some of them are only too happy to spend millions on new building or refurbishments and hire whole design teams to pick the right shade of carpet or the correct form of lighting, then they employ The Receptionist from Hell — the most miserable, sour-faced scruffily-dressed character with a total charisma by-pass — to greet their visitors.

Companies like this forget one of the basic facts of business life: it's people who matter and it's people who create the first impression of the company.

Visitors are not as alert to their surroundings as most designers would like to think. When we walk into a new firm we only get an overall impression of the decor — it's the people we tend to look at because we feel they give a good reflection of the company itself.

A negative image can be amazingly powerful and long-lasting. People rarely discuss polite staff they met at a company, but they will happily dine out on stories of rudeness and inefficiency. Ninety nine point nine per cent of a workforce may greet a visitor positively, but if just one member of staff is rude or inefficient, that is the way the company will be perceived.

Some firms spend fortunes on advertising, just to sell a particular image. All that expense is money down the drain, though, if the staff don't live up to the image that has been sold.

SCRAPING THE SURFACE

It is important to remember that a corporate image is *internal*, as well as *external*. A good image is not just some sort of a massive tarting up operation for the sake of the clients — it's a total philosophy. Scrape the veneer away and you should find a solid image lying underneath. Staff areas should be just as pleasant as the areas clients have access to. Staff should be as positive and respectful of one another as they are of visitors. We should dress as smartly for the people we work with as we do for our clients. If we don't we are telling them we don't respect them as much and that they are not worth bothering for.

A company that only tarts itself up for the client is a company that is presenting a false image.

3. self-marketing

In a perfect world we could look however we liked and people would only judge us by results and the quality of our work. Life isn't perfect, though. People who work hard and are loyal get overlooked for promotion or pay rises — while those doing a good PR job on themselves tend to get thanked and appreciated more often.

This is not to say you have to go around at work telling everyone how wonderful and how competent you are. Nobody likes a smart-ass and nobody believes a boaster. You have to *show* people how good you are — and this is where visual image can be vital.

People tend to believe what they see — telling them otherwise just doesn't work. Imagine a guy who turns up at the last minute every morning, clutching a carrier bag bursting with junk, wearing an unironed shirt with buttons missing and odd socks, and in need of a shave. Imagine his desk looks as if a grenade just hit it. Imagine every time you ask him something he looks away because he can't meet your gaze, and fiddles with his collar and clears his throat a lot.

Would you be confident he was doing his job well? Would you expect him to be efficient? If he told you he was confident in his own abilities and that he knew where everything was on his tip of a desk, would you believe him?

Image is a very powerful tool and it can work for you or against you. If the visual image belies the verbal we tend to believe what we see, rather than what we hear. If someone looks inefficient we take a lot of convincing to believe he or she is not. If someone appears impolite or uninterested we tend to go with that opinion until we're proved wrong.

A negative image invites negative prejudice that can take

a long time to disprove — it's like starting with a handicap, and an unnecessary one.

Know what it is you want to say about yourself in business and make sure that you're saying it.

Image is like learning a language — when you've mastered it you can use it to say whatever you want. Don't forget — there is no cloning going on here — your image is yours alone. Nobody is expecting you to want to say the same as everybody else in your company. Sometimes we *do* want that, though — which is where the trusty uniform comes in.

REBEL WITHOUT A CAUSE

The best image for business is the one that is appropriate for the company you work for, and the job you do (or *want* to do — remember, dress for the job you want rather than the one you've got.)

Some companies have a more traditional look, while others prefer something more casual or way-out. You wouldn't expect to see your hairdresser in a pin-stripe suit and you'd be shocked if your bank manager walked in wearing leather shorts and a t-shirt.

There is always a temptation to be a rebel, though. It's ingrained from school days. Only creeps and swots wore their uniform properly. It was good to do your own thing — it showed a healthy lack of respect for rules and authority. It was fun and the worst thing you risked was a telling off or detention.

Business is a different ball-game, though. Maybe you hate your job and you want to show that loathing visibly. Fine — sad, but fine.

Otherwise always remember what you are saying when you deliberately flaunt the expected dress or grooming codes of your company — you may be considered to be showing a lack of respect or commitment and a lack of true application to the job.

Maybe being a bit of a rebel is an appropriate plus quality for your career. Perhaps you work in a job where a little eccentricity can be a good thing. If not, think hard before you fight against conforming.

If you can dress and style yourself within the expected limits but still retain your individuality, you will have found a more winning combination.

EXERCISE

Assess the effectiveness of your own working image by running through the following checklist and counting the negatives up against the positives.

Negative Behaviour in Business:
- *Being seen turning up late.*
- *Eating breakfast at your desk.*
- *Reading a novel or a newspaper.*
- *Getting caught making private calls.*
- *Yawning a lot.*
- *Chewing gum.*
- *Grazing — continually eating at your desk — sweets, crisps, biscuits etc.*
- *Moaning a lot.*
- *Gossiping.*
- *Shouting across the office.*
- *Ignoring colleagues in the morning.*
- *Complaining about being tired after a late/drunken night.*
- *Being moody.*
- *An untidy desk.*
- *A too-tidy desk.*
- *Old coffee cups left on desk.*
- *Cuddly toys or too many desk ornaments.*
- *Old photos or postcards pinned up around desk.*
- *'Amusing' slogans: "You don't have to be mad to work here — but it helps!" etc.*
- *Plastic carrier bags.*
- *Handbags that are inappropriate for business or so full they won't close.*

- *Scruffy dress.*
- *Doodling.*

Positive Behaviour

- *Tidy, efficient-looking desk.*
- *Smiling when you greet people.*
- *Using eye contact.*
- *Looking interested.*
- *Good listening skills.*
- *Greeting colleagues positively in the morning.*
- *Carrying a businesslike bag.*
- *Dressing appropriately.*

5 body language and posture

Body language is not an exact science. Sometimes a person's movements or gestures *can* be a guide to his or her subconscious thoughts or emotions — but more often the clues can be wrong.

According to Michael Argyle of Oxford University, non-verbal signals are used to establish and maintain personal relationships, while words are used to communicate information about external events.

Studying body language will not make you a mind-reader or give you power over people by being able to analyse their deepest-hidden thoughts. What a person's body language will do, though, is speak to your subconscious — and that is why it is such a powerful communication.

PREJUDICE

Body language is one of the first factors that go to make up the all-important First Impression when we meet someone. We tend to judge people more from the way they look than from what they actually say to us — but this judgement is largely subconscious. We rarely stop to analyse why we formed an opinion about someone — if we did we would often find it based on prejudice and assumption.

A BALANCED VIEW

How are you sitting — now, as you read this book? Think about your posture. Why are you sitting like that? Probably because it's comfortable. You were thinking so hard you had moved into a certain position without being aware of how it looked.

What would your body language say to someone right now, though? Someone who didn't know you — who was seeing you for the very first time? Are your arms and legs folded? Perhaps you would look aggressive then, or remote and stand-offish. Are you slumped in your chair? If they spoke to you like that you could appear uninterested and negative.

So don't analyse *why* you do something. Instead, work out *how* it might appear to others. Then think: 'Is that what I wanted to say?' If it isn't — move.

We don't get a right to reply when our body language says the wrong thing because the communication has been silent. You may sit at a party curled up in a chair with your arms crossed, frowning, and wonder why no one came to speak to you. The others may have looked at you and got the message that you wanted to be left alone. You didn't get the chance to explain your arms were crossed because you felt cold, and you weren't frowning but just rather short-sighted.

Working on your body language to give a more positive impression does not make you a studied liar. Often it only means your image is nearer to the truth. Did you ever go out of the house in a good mood and then get told to 'cheer up' by a total stranger you passed in the street? It was your body language that was lying then — you felt happy enough but your face just happened to look rather set and miserable. Probably you were miles away, not thinking what you were doing.

Of course, you can use body language to mask more negative feelings — for instance, looking interested when you are bored witless and looking confident when you are on the point of making a run for it. If this masking is done effectively it can actually make you feel more positive, too. Like the tie or the jacket that make you feel more assertive when you wear them, body language can act as protective armour when it is used correctly.

When you lack confidence in a situation your body language will shout out to others that you are unsure of yourself. When they see these signals they will react to them. If they see confident signals they will react in a different way. If people treat you as though you are confident you will begin to feel you are, too.

LEAKAGE

Body language signals are called 'leakage' because you may try to tell someone one thing, but the truth will leak out visually.

Imagine you are at an interview. Imagine your replies to the questions are good and you are telling the interviewer how suitable you are for the job, but all the time your leg keeps rocking and you keep fiddling with your hair. These negative signals will be seen to be leaking out messages that belie your words.

The same can happen when we practise customer care. We might say the right things to the client when we greet them — but a surly expression will leave a negative impression.

This will also happen when we show a lack of sincerity. People who have to greet clients on a regular basis often begin to lack sincerity after a while. Their verbal greetings may be the same but their smiles may be too bright and fixed and their eyes glassy. The positive message will become eroded by this visible falseness.

As a rough guide try to avoid the following negative leakage:

LOOKING NERVOUS

- Crossed arms and/or legs
- Carrying books or papers across your chest

- Slumped posture
- Sitting perched on the edge of the chair
- Wringing hands
- Tapping foot
- Rocking leg
- Drumming fingers
- Biting nails
- Fiddling with jewellery or hair
- Covering your mouth with your hand when you talk
- Rocking in your chair
- Scratching a lot
- Clearing your throat too much
- Straightening tie
- Playing with watch or cufflinks
- Hands in pockets

LOOKING AGGRESSIVE

- Arms folded across chest
- Staring
- Pointing
- Making a fist
- Leaning over someone

BEING RUDE

- Working while someone is talking to you
- Puffing
- Tutting
- Smirking
- Whispering
- Cracking knuckles
- Grooming yourself
- Standing too close
- Packing up papers and folders before the meeting has finished
- Shaking hands too hard
- Limp handshakes
- Yawning
- Looking at watch

ON THE FIDDLE

We all have our own pet fiddle — or nervous, comfort gesture. Often we are unaware of the habit and genuinely surprised when someone points it out. Find out what your pet fiddle is — it is probably the strongest form of negative leakage you are using. Maybe you do a couple of things or more when you get tense. See if any of these sound familiar:

- Blinking a lot.
- Fiddling with rings, watches, earrings, chains.

- Pushing glasses up the nose
- Tapping or clicking pens
- Playing with paper clips.
- Jingling money in pocket.
- Picking at fingernails.

- Twiddling bits of hair.
- Smoking.

You may not do these things because you're nervous but they will make you look nervous, all the same.

ACTION POINT

Identify your negative gestures and try not to do them at moments when it counts — eg, a presentation, meeting, interview etc. If you're not sure what you do ask a colleague — they'll only be too pleased to tell you.

GESTURES

A lot of us speak with our hands. Some people claim they couldn't talk at all if their arms were clamped down to their sides. Gestures can be useful as long as we have control over their conversation. If they endorse our words they will add emphasis and interest. If they're acting as leakage, though, and contradicting our desired message, then we're in trouble.

People seeing themselves on video or tv are surprised by what they see. Often we don't even recognise ourselves on the screen — that's because we're seeing ourselves as others see us for the very first time. It's a shock — and rightly so. When else did you get to see your gestures and your expressions?

We see our arms waving like windmills or our feet tapping out some subconscious rhythm and we come up with the classic comment: 'I didn't know I did that!'

The trouble is, others did. Colleagues have known for years — only we were ignorant. Still — we're not going to see ourselves as stars of the video screen again in a hurry, so why worry? This is the famous ostrich technique — stick your head in the sand — ignore it and don't look and it will always go away — right?

Of course the fact is that if we refuse to acknowledge these gestures, they won't go away at all — it's just that we won't see them again. The more professional line to take is to find out all we can about them and see what needs keeping and what needs editing from the repertoire.

Our bodies should dance in time with our words — when they fall out of step we need a rethink. Gestures will be irritating to others if they are too persistent. They will also be annoying if they look too pompous. There are in addition 'trendy' gestures that can be as aggravating as trendy words. (When did you last see someone hanging airquotes round every other word and want to smack him or her right on the nose?)

POMPOUS GESTURES

- Head tilted back when you talk.
- Eyes closed when you talk.
- Looking down your nose.
- Peering over the top of glasses.
- Waving glasses about when you talk.

- Steepling the fingers.
- Thumbs tucked in braces.
- Pursed mouth.

These are often accompanied by phrases like:

'I understand what you're trying to say . . . but . . .'
'That's all very well, but . . .'
'In the fullness of time . . .'

DAFT GESTURES

- Flapping hands around as you talk
- Undoing and then doing up jacket buttons or watch straps.
- Things on chains that go in the mouth or over the chin, or dangle from the nose.
- Wringing hands.
- Wiping hands across face.
- Tearing paper into little balls.
- Cleaning ears or nails.
- Banging the table instead of laughing when someone tells a joke.
- Shoes hanging off toe or off feet altogether.
- Chewing pens.
- Airquotes, thumbs up, doing the letter T when you want some tea, anything rude!

POSITIVE GESTURES

- Open hand gestures.
- Carrying documents to one side, rather than clutched to the chest.

- Keeping the thumb out when you put your hands in your pockets — that way you won't stuff them too far inside.
- Good listening gestures — eye contact, tilting the

head, nodding to encourage speech, leaning forward slightly.

USEFUL GESTURES

Gestures can help us to be polite when we are unable to speak. If you are busy on the phone, for instance, and visitors arrive, you can acknowledge them politely with a nod and maybe one finger held up to show 'one minute!' instead of ignoring them until you are free.

You can also use gesture to be more assertive. If a colleague constantly interrupts you when you are on the phone you might raise the flat of your hand towards them in a 'stop' gesture to get them to wait. Whereas, if you just look away and do nothing they will try harder to interrupt.

TERRITORY AND TOUCH

We all have our own invisible circle of territory around us and feel uncomfortable if someone we don't know breaches that circle. It's our space and we are fiercely defensive of it.

'Important' people tend to be allotted more personal space, which is why being crowded can make us feel belittled and inferior, leading to anxiety or aggression. Invaded space is something we find impossible to talk about, though, however uncomfortable it makes us feel. In tests done in America a volunteer deliberately sat within the 'comfort zone' of strangers in a public space. The only reactions of those strangers were to turn away, display anxiety, or even walk away completely. Not one person asked the volunteer to move.

When we move about we move within four distance

bands, each one defined by the discomfort we feel when that band is breached.

The furthest band is the public band. At this distance we are comfortable with most strangers. If you were talking in public this is the distance you would feel most comfortable to have between you and the audience.

Then comes the social band. This is the distance we keep between ourselves and people we know, but not very well.

The third band is the friendly band — the sort of gap we would keep between ourselves and people at a party or in a pub.

The nearest band is the intimate band — and this is reserved for lovers and close family members.

When someone invades the wrong band or territory it makes us feel extremely uncomfortable, even if we go to great pains to hide that discomfort. When someone invades our intimate band without invitation we feel acute discomfort because the signals we receive are of a sexual or physical threat. Our bodies prepare for the 'fight or flight' response — the breathing quickens, the heart starts pumping faster and the adrenalin pours into the bloodstream. To mask our discomfort we will often smile more. Interrogators often use similar techniques to browbeat their victim.

Only invade another's intimate space if you're absolutely sure it's appropriate. The friendly arm around the shoulder or seat pulled close may be done for the best of motives but it could have disastrous results.

Your desk becomes part of that territory, and so does your chair. You'll feel annoyed and uncomfortable if someone puts his or her things on your desk or sits on your chair without asking.

We're forced to invade others' territory every day. Travelling to work on a crowded train or bus or getting into a full lift means we are too close for comfort — but we can cope with that as long as the subconscious body language rules are observed.

To acknowledge you've invaded another's space and show you mean no threat you have to stare into space and make minimal movement. People in the lift will stand straight and look intently at the floor numbers. Commuters will go out of their way not to make eye contact with one another.

Balance is vital in situations like this and any imbalance of eye contact, smiling, distance and leaning can lead to an approach and avoidance situation, where one party will be invasive while the other is forced into retreat.

If we sit or stand too close to someone, we normally try to redress the balance by lessening other signs of intimacy, like eye contact.

It is also forbidden to touch without permission, even accidentally. Two people brushing past each other will both apologise for the inadvertent contact.

Touch breaks down barriers though — so a kind of 'permitted touching system' has been invented for business and social use. We do this in business via the handshake. It is the only form of touch considered appropriate, especially on first meeting.

The handshake, then, becomes a bit of a loaded dice. Who extends his or her hand first? How strong should the grip be? Who do you shake hands with? Some men even think it inappropriate to shake hands with a woman. If you're nervous about meeting someone you'll know all about the dreaded sweaty palm syndrome.

In business it is the person doing the greeting who should instigate the handshake, or the one in the superior position. The handshake should always take place using the right hand and it should vary in firmness, depending on the one you are receiving. You should not grab someone's arm as you shake their hand and you should use eye contact.

Two-handed shakes are a bit too earnest, especially on first meeting.

And — don't wipe a sweaty palm on the leg of your trousers or skirt just as you make your approach — a furtive dab with a tissue or some cologne is much more attractive!

Touch is variable, according to culture and nationality. Sidney Jourard of The University of Florida watched people talking together in public and counted the times they touched in the space of one hour. In Puerto Rico it was 180 touches, in Paris 110 and in London zero.

POWER-POSTURING

Did you ever feel suddenly subordinate in a colleague's company? Do some people drain you of all confidence the minute you meet them? Do you have more trouble being assertive with some people than others? The chances are you're a victim of Power-Posturing.

Power-posturing is nasty. It means using the sort of body language and behaviour that is guaranteed to make the other person feel inferior. Some people do it deliberately — others just seem to have been born that way. Either way it's stupid and offensive, yet some companies seem to have power-posturing built into their culture.

The symptoms of power-posturing can vary from general aloofness to shouting, swearing and out-and-out bullying. It's lowering behaviour, guaranteed to make the minions stay in their place.

Bad interviewers will often go in for bouts of it. They remember how humble they felt when they were job-hunting and they want to make applicants suffer the same sort of torture. They're top dog now and — boy, do they want to make sure you know it.

Such an interviewer will sit on the biggest, leather-clad, high-backed chair and an entire rainforest will have been decimated to make the desk her or she is lounging behind. The chair will have its back to a window, so that the sun pours from behind the interviewer's head in god-like rays, to make sure you have trouble seeing his or her face properly.

An interviewer of this kind will not know your name, and will carry on working when you first walk in, showing exactly how low down his or her list of priorities you come.

When you knock on the door, he or she will yell out 'Come!' and you will feel as though you are back at school.

Other favourite power-posturing techniques include:

- Standing behind someone's chair and reading over his or her shoulder while he or she works.
- Leaning over someone's desk.
- Sitting on someone's desk.

- Staying slumped in your chair when you greet someone.
- Giving the 'Top-dog' handshake — ie, twisting your hand on top when you shake.
- Giving the pincer-grip handshake, effectively crushing your victim's hand.
- Standing too close when you talk to someone.

- Smoking in someone else's space.
- Shouting orders.
- Swearing.
- Continuing to work when colleagues talk to you.

- Drumming the tips of your fingers together when you listen to them.
- Leaning back in your chair with your hands behind your head.
- Sitting with your feet on your desk.
- Staring.
- Any uninvited, inappropriate touch.
- Ignoring people when they greet you.
- Going into meetings or lectures with your pager or portable phone switched on, except in the most urgent cases (eg an on-call heart surgeon).

ACTION POINTS

So what can a victim of power-posturing do about it? Well, perhaps the most useful thing is to recognise it in the first place. Pinpointing the techniques used will often take some of the sting out of them.

If you're confronted by a terminal power-posturer the best technique is to move as little as possible (you'll only look twitchy and nervous) and smile in a knowing, confident way. This will let them know their little game is not working.

Don't ever start questioning yourself. Once they make you start doubting your self-worth they have won — game, set and match. Only confront them after some careful thought and never lose your temper or get upset. The constant snooper for instance (the one who stands reading over your shoulder while you work) could be dealt with pleasantly but firmly:

'Look — I know you don't mean to make me feel uncomfortable, but I find it difficult to work while you are watching.' etc.

People who stand too close to talk to you can be stopped with the right body language. Look them straight in the eye when they hover, take a step back and then let your eyes measure the gap that is left between you before looking back at them again. They should get the message.

If someone ignores you when you greet him or her in the

morning, go right on greeting him or her every morning in the same polite and confident way. Don't stop and don't let your tone get sarcastic. His or her attitude and lack of response is his or her own problem — you should not allow it to affect your own normal manners or behaviour.

Never greet rudeness with rudeness — that will only lead to a 'no-win' situation.

POSITIVE POSTURE

When we work we usually sit, and when we sit for too long we tend to slump. If you stand a lot at work you'll probably slump in the upright position — it's very hard not to when your back's aching or your legs are tired. Slumping looks negative, though — as well as being bad for the posture long-term. The more you stoop the more you'll need to, and the worse your posture will get.

Most office chairs are either badly designed for correct support or so old they no longer do the job properly. It's important to keep an eye on your posture, though — not just for the look of it but for the sake of your health, too.

QUICK-FIX POSTURE TECHNIQUES

When you find your spine getting tired, spend a few seconds to get your posture back with this simple alignment exercise:

1. Stand up with your arms down by your sides. Place your feet a few inches apart and make sure your weight is evenly balanced.
2. Stand straight on your feet — too often we tend to stand on the outside edges — and gently rock backwards and forwards until your weight is evenly balanced between the ball and the heel of the foot.
3. Make sure your legs are straight and pitch the pelvis in and under slightly so that that is straight, too. (This will stop you arching your back.)
4. Straighten your spine from the neck and try to touch the ceiling with the top of your head.
5. Bring the shoulders back — not by arching the spine, but by rotating them in a circle, up, round and back, until they are back and down.
6. Hold that pose for a few seconds. Because your posture is straighter you can breathe properly again, taking air into the full length of your lung. Rotate the shoulders a few times more and it will have the effect of a massage, alleviating stress. In a few seconds you will look and feel more positive and less tired. The more times you do this exercise during the day, the less time you will spend slumped.

Another good exercise if you sit a lot at work is to raise the feet together, a few inches off the ground and rotate them in circles from the ankle. This exercises the stomach muscles, helps to stop the feet and legs aching, and improves circulation in the feet.

Stretching is good, but bad for your personal image because — unfortunately — we equate it with just having woken up. Try some serious stretches in the loo, instead of at your desk.

TAKING POSITIVE STEPS

Try to improve your walk to become more positive. How are you walking now?

Passively Eyes down, shoulders hunched and hands stuffed in pockets? Or maybe clinging on to the strap of your handbag? Do you have your arms permanently folded or carry papers or files clutched across your chest? Do you look down all the time when you walk?

Aggressively Large strides, thumping feet, arms swinging with hands into fists? Frowning, with too much eye contact?

Fussily Pottering about with hands wringing at waist-level? Quick, small steps? A nervous, over-anxious smile?

Cockily Bouncy strides, chin up, looking about constantly for attention and approval? Hands sometimes thrust into pockets but with a shoulder swing that implies arrogance, rather than insecurity?

Thoughtful Head down, hands clasped behind back? A slow pace, posture slightly bent forward?

An *assertive*, confident walk is one with the back straight, head up and arms swinging freely. It is also quite fast-paced, implying you are busy on important business. The feet should never scuff and you should avoid high heels that give the impression of teetering.

SITTING IT OUT

The way we sit depends pretty much on the shape of the chair we use and the type of work we are doing. Like the walk, though, it's difficult not to attempt to read someone's state of mind from his or her sitting position.

Slump The slump can look passive-aggressive. If someone comes to talk to you and you don't respond in an interested way, you will offend him or her. Staying slumped in your chair will have this effect, and if you use the chair in a rocking movement the insult will have been doubled.

Try selling a product or an idea to someone who is slumped in his or her seat studying his or her hands or feet, and you'll understand just how obstructive the position can be. Quite often the one doing the slumping can be asserting his or her authority in a negative way. If the slumped person leans back, with hands behind his or her head, the power-posturing signals will increase even more. This position will often be accompanied by a confident smile.

The Double-Cross Sitting with your legs crossed won't look unduly defensive unless you fold your arms as well. Some people look tense because they appear to be holding their own arms or legs when they sit.

If you cross your legs at the ankle you may look prim and old-fashioned. Crossing one leg over the other so that the ankle is resting on the knee, though, will look confident to the point of power-posturing.

It would be very difficult to sell while your arms were folded or you were leaning back in your seat. Someone trying to inject conviction into his or her tone would do better to lean forward and use open gestures.

The Disappearing Act When we're nervous we wish we could vanish — and this is often apparent in the way we sit. Maybe you're hiding behind a large bag you have on your lap, or ducking behind a big desk. Your feet will be tucked away under your seat, implying you would rather be hiding down there, too — or they may be trying to make an early exit, pointing towards the door.

Insecurity shows in the way we perch on the edge of a seat or even start to bind ourselves around it, tucking our feet round the chair legs and our hands around the arms as though we expect to be tipped out at any minute.

The Thinker Elbows in place on the arms of the chair, hands loosely clasped, leaning slightly forward, nodding but otherwise still — this position will give the impression we're listening carefully. Animals and humans tend to cock their heads slightly when they're listening to something they want to hear.

If you hold your hand to your face you will look judgemental. The classic poses for this are the finger horizontal across the top lip, implying you're going to listen, rather than talk; the hands clasped with the two index fingers steepled beneath the chin, implying decision-making; or the finger on the cheek that will give much the same look. A man will appear thoughtful if he strokes his beard.

Disagreement When we're listening to a speaker we may show any disagreement in several different ways. The most common is the narrowing of the eyes, sometimes followed by a glance away, often at the ceiling. We may move from a leaning forward, listening pose, to a more distancing posture and our hands might join across our waists if the point is carried on.

Some people signal their disagreement by the obvious head-shaking, though others might be more subtle in an attempt to be polite. A frown will often do, or they may take their glasses off and place the tip of one arm against their lips. If your listener closes his or her eyes and rubs the bridge of his or her nose, you can assume you've gone too far with your point.

Indifference or Annoyance Irritation is often easy to spot — listeners will often begin quick, repetitive movements, like tapping a foot, drumming their fingers or clicking a pen. Sighing, folding your arms, studying your watch or looking away will all imply the same thing. Chewing gum annoys people because it implies arrogance or indifference. Sharing food is different, though — it's the solitary aspect of the gum-chewing that makes it such an insult.

Reassurance or Comfort When we're lacking confidence we send out visual signals as we reach around for reassurance. Often these will be comfort gestures, like touching or stroking. Earlobes are comfort zones to touch and so is the back of the neck. Touching or stroking the hair is a calming movement.

When we say something we're not sure about, we often clutch at our necks or cover our mouths with our hands. A woman might fiddle with a necklace, or a man straighten his tie continually.

Biting or chewing is another comfort manoeuvre. When we were young we might have sucked our thumbs, but as we get older that may advance to nail-biting or pen-chewing.

Superiority Often a chair will denote superiority just as much as the person sitting in it. Some bosses like big chairs. They like padded leather, preferably black, and they like high backs and big arms. The chairs will have a big lean-back facility, tilting easily into the prone position. Nobody can show superiority on a low, rickety chair with no arms.

The ultimate in superior sitting is the feet-on-the-desk pose. In the same vein is the tilt-back and gestures such as pointing or the hands flat on the desk.

Eye contact is important for superiority, as can be the handshake and any other form of touch. Too much eye contact will be challenging and aggressive. People using it will give the impression they are staking their claim to their position in the pecking order. No eye contact can look dismissive. Handshakes may be turned into power-grips, with the one who gets his or her hand on top winning the combat. Touch can be used to show superiority, too. Some people adopt a parent/child pose with people they consider their subordinates. A friendly arm round the shoulder or a hand on the arm may look like reassurance but it can often be a reminder who's in charge.

PACK MENTALITY

We all like to run with the pack now and again and, in business, that pack means our work colleagues. People wandering into our companies will tend to see us firstly as a pack and only secondly as individuals. If one member of that pack is sending out the wrong body language signals, we will all get blamed because bad signals scream out louder than good ones.

The leader of the pack is often the one with the authority and we like to mirror his or her body language as much as possible. It is often easy to pick the highest-ranking member of staff at a meeting because he or she will tend to change position first and most of the others will gradually follow suit.

In large groups we like to remain anonymous. As commuters we are part of a huge herd, moving from A to B with as little fuss as possible. It is difficult to get any member of this herd to act as an individual because the group instinct takes over. If there is an 'incident' en route we tend to keep our heads down and ignore it. Evacuating large crowds in an emergency can take time because herds are slow to decide and slow to move — nobody wants to be the first one to make a move when the fire alarms go off.

SUMMARY POINTS

1. *Study your own body language and evaluate the signals it will be sending to colleagues and clients.*
2. *Avoid any negative communications and any 'leakage'.*
3. *Make sure you're not power-posturing, and deal assertively with anyone who is.*
4. *Practise your listening skills — show that you're listening and encourage other people to talk.*

---

6 face facts

Of course you can't see the look on your face — you're on the wrong side of your eyeballs. You may think you're looking wonderfully alert and intelligent but other people may tell a different story. Facial expressions are even more open to misinterpretation than body language.

We use masking a lot more in business than we do in our social lives — trying to look interested when we're bored, knowledgeable when we don't have a clue, and polite when we dislike the person we're having to deal with.

If your job means coping with the public on a daily basis, you will be well acquainted with qualities like tolerance and patience. We all need to use a little customer care now and again and we've all heard the phrase: 'The customer is always right.' What it means, of course, is that we have to *pretend* they're right, even when we know they're not. It is at this point that the corporate smile will come into play — and a fearsome sight it is, too.

Smiles that look false are dreadful. People who have to employ them on a regular, long-term basis — such as politicians and greeters at exhibitions — often end up displaying a terrifying rictus that drives clients away screaming into the night.

When an animal bares its teeth it is showing aggression — and that is what we unwittingly display if the smile looks too fake. The teeth are on display but the eyes are dead — the lights are on but there's no one at home.

If your job entails smiling through thick and thin, you should at least practise that grin until it becomes natural and sincere-looking. Otherwise don't bother. The trick is to smile with your eyes as well as your mouth. Try it. Look at yourself in the mirror. You have been warned.

Most of us have two major facial expressions — smiling or miserable. Unfortunately the older we get the more these two become extremes. Skin starts to droop, frown lines set in, laughter lines look like creases of utter misery. When we smile, the effort of lifting all that sagging flesh becomes greater each year.

Face lifts may sound like the solution but too many and too tight and they can stretch the skin back into a permanent expression of alarm.

All you have to do is to remember to compensate. Look in the mirror a lot. Faces in repose will usually look miserable. Find ways of looking serious and businesslike instead of depressed. Don't be embarrassed — actors do it, so why shouldn't you? Raise an eyebrow. Try looking amused. Now try cynical. Why not have a go at sexy? Feel the muscles working. Check out the results. Practise. See what looks good.

There's no dishonesty in a little self-discovery. Much worse to look permanently worried or anxious without knowing it.

SEEING EYE-TO-EYE

Eye contact is a powerful tool. Use too little and you'll look nervous or even shifty. Use too much and you'll appear overpowering and aggressive.

Looking people in the eye is a bit like breathing — it's something we do without thinking about it. When it's brought to our attention, though, we find it difficult to maintain.

How much eye contact do you use in business? Do a one-day check-up — you'll be surprised at the results. Study the eye contact of your colleagues, too. Do they use more than you, or less? Do you use more with some people than others — if so, why? How much eye contact do you use when you're listening to people or greeting clients?

Like the strength of the handshake or the amount you smile, you'll find your eye contact will vary depending on who you are dealing with.

Some people are awkward to look straight in the eye — usually because they either use either too much eye contact or not enough. If they spend most of their time with their eyes to the floor during the conversation, with only quick glances in our direction, we will be empathetic and look at them less. If they stare us out, though, we may feel embarrassed and look away more quickly.

Facial expressions are important because it is the face we spend the most time looking at when we are talking to one another. During a conversation people will look at one another on average between one and two thirds of the time. If they spend more than two thirds of the time gazing then the chances are they're in love.

When you are made to feel uncomfortable by a conversation or question you will tend to look away, but if you become aggressive your eye contact will probably increase.

During a natural conversation we will use more eye contact when we are listening than when we are speaking. This gives the impression we are listening intently and speaking honestly. If you look away when someone is talking to you and then stare when you give your reply, you will give the impression of being bored by the other person's points and glib when you make your own.

Sometimes our eyes stray to other parts of the face during a conversation. If we stay around the eye area we should be OK. Look at the mouth too much and you will either look as though you're flirting or studying a piece of spinach stuck between the other person's teeth. Gaze at the end of the nose and you'll bring out all sorts of paranoia in him or her.

EYE CONTACT EXERCISES

It is a good idea to increase your eye contact in business, especially if you lack confidence or assertive skills. The trick is not to overdo it, though. Try a few of these exercises to help to increase that eye contact more comfortably.

1. *Stare your dog out. (Yes, you might make him twitchy, but it's easier to start with pets than humans. If you can't even meet the dog's gaze you will know you have serious insecurity problems.)*
2. *Stare yourself out. Look in the mirror and tell yourself out loud that you're confident — really confident. See who looks away first.*
3. *Find a friend you feel comfortable with (no laughing) and take it in turns to ask and reply to simple requests using eye contact. Then role-play more difficult scenarios, like asking to borrow money or confessing to a ten-year affair with the friend's partner.*
4. *When you greet someone new in business hold eye contact all the way through the verbal greeting and don't rush your words. Smile at the same time — you don't want to come across as aggressive.*
5. *When you talk to colleagues call them by their names and don't start speaking until they've met your gaze. (Don't be too strict about this one — more nervous colleagues may feel uncomfortable — try it on the more confident types first.)*

7 dress to impress

the top ten tips

1. BUY LESS — PAY MORE

Work wardrobes should not be vast and unwieldy. Impulse buys are not a good idea. This is part of your job and your career — an important part. Take control of it and approach your buying with the same professional, critical eye you use at work.

It is better to have four useful, good quality suits than it is to have a rail full of cheap bargains that neither say the right thing nor coordinate. No one is asking you to pay more in the long term; in fact, you will probably end up saving money.

2. LOOK AFTER WHAT YOU HAVE

Clothes that are well-made should have a good shelf-life but even the best quality garments will suffer early fatigue if you don't look after them.

Treat your business clothes well and they'll last longer. Maintenance routines should consist of:

- Buying good-quality hangers. The metal ones ruin your clothes.
- Investing in a good clothes brush and a dry-cleaning spot spray.
- Having a sewing kit to hand at all times and knowing how to sew on buttons and do instant repairs.
- Getting suits cleaned regularly and re-textured every so often.
- Emptying pockets at night.
- Using an umbrella. If a suit gets wet it is ruined, yet your frequently see businessmen darting about in

their office suits in the rain. The shape goes and the interfacing will never look the same.
- Learning how to iron properly. Never place an iron straight onto the suit because it will go shiny, and nobody wants a satin business suit. Cover it with a clean damp cloth first.
- Stuff shoes with tissue — they keep their shape longer — and always use boot-trees.
- Don't cover light-coloured garments with plastic bags — the static attracts the dirt. Use cloth covers, instead.
- Read labels before you clean things.

3. AVOID HIGH FASHION

What must come in must go out — avoid the latest looks unless you either work in the fashion business or have won the national lottery. Most new looks have a three-month life-span. You will probably want your business clothes to last a couple of years at least. Remember wide lapels or flares or those over-sized suits of the eighties? Men rarely follow fashion for business and that's the sort of time-warp disaster they get stuck with when they do. Now they tend to wear classics. Women should take note.

4. AVOID POWER-DRESSING

Power-dressing was all the rage in the Eighties. A lot of people made a lot of money very quickly and started this look. Then they lost all their money. The look is equated with failure, not success. This is the Caring Nineties. Avoid the look at all costs.

5. TEST CLOTHES BEFORE YOU BUY.

Ask yourself the following questions in the fitting room:

Does it fit? Only you will know this. Don't be fooled by an admiring salesperson. Don't buy something too small just so that you can tell everyone that's the size you got into.

Is it suitable? You know your job, you know your company — is it right? Is it appropriate? Never buy for social use then wear it for work when you're fed up with it.

Does it suit me? Is the colour right? Does the shape
flatter? Colours will affect your skin tone and some will
enhance while others will make you look dreadful. Hold the
fabric next to your face and see what the effect is. You
should not just buy what *you* like, but what *likes you*, too.

Shapes are important. If you are short you should stick
to neater, slimmer lines. Long skirts will make you look
tiny and so will double-breasted suits with turn-ups, on a
man. Taller women can look wrong in shorter skirts and
cropped jackets.

6. BE COMFORTABLE

Buying uncomfortable clothes is stupid. We should wear
things that look good and feel good, too. So why do we buy
shoes that are too tight, trousers a size too small, skirts
with splits we can neither walk in nor sit down in, shoes
with heels so high they make us walk badly? Who knows?
But we do. Comfortable clothes don't have to look like
shapeless sacks. A good suit can be comfortable if it fits
OK. Move around in the changing room. Bend, sit, raise
your arms and see what happens. Screw some of the fabric
up in your hand and see if it creases. You're going to spend
a lot of time in that outfit — you need to see how it will
wear.

7. CUSTOMIZE CLOTHES

Buy cheap but look dear. Most cheap clothes only look
cheap because of the way they're finished. Buy on a budget
if you want to but then customize for a more expensive
look.

On an inexpensive garment the buttons will often be
tacky, the belt will be either plastic or a self belt and the
hems will have been stitched by machine. Changing
buttons is one of the easiest ways to give a jacket new life.
A plain blazer may come with matching buttons or plastic
buttons. Swap them for some brass buttons and see how
much more stunning the jacket looks. Try some other
buttons in summer and you'll feel as though you're wearing
a new jacket.

Buy inexpensive leather belts to make skirts or trousers look better and re-hem them properly so that the finishing looks good.

The right accessories will make a difference, too. Buy a good tie, even if the suit is cheap. Try scarves or a necklace or matching tights to give an outfit extra impact. Update your spectacles as often as you can. Styles change more frequently these days and a modern pair will give the right image. Take a friend whose taste you admire along for a second opinion when you choose the frames.

Shop in the designer shops to get an idea of style for your clothes, and then buy cheaper copies of the same look. If you want designer labels keep your eyes open for bargains. Lots of the top designers have end of season showroom sales that they advertise in newspapers and there is a current plan to copy the American idea of opening warehouses that sell cut-price designer wear direct to the public. Don't just buy something because it's a bargain, though. Make sure you know roughly how much those clothes would have cost full-price and check they're what you need, too.

Co-ordinate the colours of your business wardrobe. If you're planning on a shoe-string pick one colour from the business spectrum (make sure it's *your* colour — one that suits you and one you feel good in, too) and use that as your base colour. Buy suits, skirts or trousers in that colour and then work around it with co-ordinates. Invest in good-quality leather shoes and buy basic black, unless you have enough to spend on colours.

8. FIT FOR BUSINESS

All clothes look cheap if they fit badly — even top-price designer suits. Ignore the size on the label — every shop has its own interpretation of measurements and sizing. Buy slightly bigger rather than too tight if you can't get a perfect fit. If it's pulling at the seams leave it on the rack — don't plan to diet to get into it. Shops have always been notorious for stocking unrealistic sizes and shapes but fortunately several are opening departments for extra large or small sizes now and there are more specialist shops appearing on the high street. If you don't see what you want, though — write to the head office. Shops are only businesses, after all and — like most other businesses — they work on supply and demand. If you don't tell them what you want then they won't know you're looking.

Once you've bought your suit or skirt and jacket, see if it needs altering to get a perfect fit. If you're not handy on the sewing machine take it to a dry cleaning shop that does alterations. The money spent getting sleeves turned up or down or darts taken in is money well spent because it will make your garments look twice the price.

9. BAGS OF FUN

Your choice of business dress may say a lot about you but the bag you're using for work will speak volumes. A good business bag is the quickest fix your visual image can get. Even someone dressed casually will look professional if they carry a briefcase, but an overstuffed handbag or a plastic carrier will ruin the look of the most businesslike suit. Here's a rough guide to the language of your bag:

Small Handbag Neat, pedantic. Perfectionist. Not a corporate animal. Fussy.

Overflowing Handbag Messy, untidy. Creative. Muddled thinking.

Wicker Basket County lady type. Gets purse stolen frequently and ladders other womens' tights on the train. More into baking buns than handling business deals.

Ethnic Bags/Rucksacks Student type. Not yet evolved into corporate animal.

Plastic Carrier Bag Total non-professional image. Housework comes first — business not even second. The sort of person who does everything at the last minute. A disaster at self-marketing and a walking advert for the local supermarket.

Posh Shop Carrier Bag OK, so you once shopped at Fortnum's/Harrods/Joseph and you've been ironing out that same carrier bag every night since then. Do you really think you're impressing anyone, though?

Corporate Carrier Bag Tacky-looking, unless you really did get an unexpectedly huge bunch of documents to take home with you that night. Companies who use them are projecting a supermarket image.

Plastic, hard-sided Briefcases Un-stylish. Go with white socks and Crimplene trousers.

Leather Briefcases Businesslike. High-status. Implies you take work home with you. No one sees the newspaper and apple inside until you open it on the train.

Old Leather Briefcases with Flip-Over Clasp Look very cool worn with a good modern suit. Otherwise the sort of beaten-leather things that tweedy schoolteachers used to throw into the back of Morris Minors.

Big, Zip-Top Portfolios Dull. Not enough work. Only use in emergencies.

10. HAIR APPARENT

Grooming is the ultimate accessory to your outfit. Did your hairstyle get stuck in a rut? When did you last think of changing it? Always make sure your hair is well groomed and up-to-date, without being way-out. Women in more traditional companies should avoid wild, flowing locks. Try to keep hair sleek and tie it back if it's long. Men working for the same types of firms should keep hair short and well-cut.

groomed for success

The clothes we wear can be changed on a daily basis but our faces, bodies and hair can't.

Someone who is well groomed will look good in almost any outfit but someone who is scruffy, with oily hair, will look bad in even the most expensive designer suit.

Good maintenance is cheap and easy to do once you work it into your daily routine. Like a good diet and a healthy lifestyle, it is an essential component of a positive image.

QUICK TIPS FOR MEN AND WOMEN

Get enough sleep.
Stop smoking.
Cut down alcohol consumption.
Eat a healthy balanced diet.
Take regular, non-competitive enjoyable exercise.
Cut out caffeine.

WHEN IN DOUBT?

Cloning an image can suppress individuality and dressing like all your colleagues can be boring. Your style of businesswear should reflect your own tastes as well as the image of your company. Different jobs require different styles of dress and within that corporate look there is usually room for some healthy diversity. Even some of the larger City companies known for their more traditional dress code have recently been adopting a 'Weekend casual wear on a Friday' policy. Some companies prefer casual dress all week because it is more appropriate to the job and the client.

If you understand the culture of your company it should be easy enough to fit inside its dress code parameters. Sometimes, though - maybe for an interview with a new firm, or a meeting with a client - it is good to be aware of the more traditional ideas of suitable business dress. This would be the sort of 'business uniform' that would be the safe option for most occasions.

TRADITIONAL CLASSIC WEAR FOR MEN;

'A man should look as if he had bought his clothes with intelligence, put them on with care, and then forgotten all about them.' - Hardy Amies.

<u>SUIT</u> Blue or Grey. Plain fabric (no man-made fibres) or a light pin-stripe. Charcoal or navy are always safe colours.

Black is not a good buy as it would be considered unsuitable in more formal businesses.

<u>CUT</u> Cut and fit are important. Trousers shouldn't drop below the waistline and the back flap of the jacket should hang closed when you wear it - not stick out horizontally.

Trousers should be worn with a plain leather belt or braces.

They should have a good straight crease front and back and break once only before hitting the shoe at the front of the foot and cover three-quarter of the shoe at the back.

Turn-ups (if worn) should be de-fluffed regularly.

If your pocket-lining shows when you sit down the trousers are too tight.

Jacket sleeves should be the right length and allow half an inch of shirt cuff to show.

Double-breasted jackets should be worn with the inside button done-up.

Single breasted jackets should be worn with either the top button (two-buttoned jacket) done up, or the middle button (three-buttoned).

Blazers look smart but are still considered a bit daring in more traditional businesses.

SHIRTS

Shirts should be cotton poplin, with either plain or button-down collars, but make sure the collar has been ironed to lie flat and not curl.

The sign of a good shirt is the number of pleats at the cuff - the more pleats the better the shirt. Another sign is the split seam at the shoulder yoke. Cufflinks look good, but only on fold-back cuffs.

TIES

Ties create the greatest area of self-expression for the businessman, but make sure that the message you're giving out is one you will want to send out all day. If you meet clients from a variety of careers you can always keep a drawerful of appropriate looks.

Ties should be worn so that the tip comes half-way across the belt buckle, or slightly longer for a more modern look.

The thin end shouldn't show.

The two most popular knots for ties are the Four-in-Hand and the Windsor.

The most classic ties are made from silk and bright colours are, by tradition, not worn with a business suit, although that rule is probably the most commonly broken these days.

A good tie is cut on the cross, which makes it hang well. To see if it is, hold it up by its thin end and see if it hangs without twisting.

The stripe should traditionally run from the left shoulder downwards.

TRADITIONAL CLASSICS FOR WOMEN

JACKETS:

A jacket or blazer is ideal traditional business wear. Try to pick fabrics that hang well, like fine wool or crepe, and check it won't crease easily before you buy.

A skirt and shirt is o.k. if you're working on a limited budget.

Navy is the classic colour. Deep red is fine and so is charcoal or even chocolate brown. Women can wear a far wider spectrum than men and still be considered suitable. Patterned jackets are o.k. though you may get bored more quickly.

SUITS:

Are fine and you can mix or match the jackets with other skirts.

SKIRTS:

Should be knee-length or longer for a traditional look. When you buy a skirt check it moves well and sits well. See what happens to the splits when you walk.

TROUSERS:

Some firms still don't approve. Tailored trousers only for formal business wear.

TOPS:

Shirts or bodices under jackets and nothing too low-cut.

TIGHTS:

At all times for formal business wear. Sheer texture and neutral colours or black with a black skirt or shoes.

SHOES:

Low or medium heel court shoe. Black is easiest.

8 bad behaviour – a guide to modern business etiquette

"The way staff behave towards one another is a gauge of the effectiveness of an organisation. If we treat one another badly, that will come across to clients, even if we treat them well." — Coopers & Lybrand.

manners

Does etiquette exist in the office of the Nineties? Hopefully it does, because etiquette is a good way to get business done smoothly and efficiently with positive feelings on all sides.

Bad manners are self-reproducing. Be rude to someone and the chances are they'll be just as rude to the next person they meet. Be polite and helpful, though, and they'll pass those qualities on just as readily.

We're the same when we're driving — if we get cut up we go off snarling and cursing, but if someone lets us through with a smile we'll feel more generous when it's our turn to queue.

Managers should take note. If they use lowering behaviour on their staff those same colleagues will either copy the behaviour when they're dealing with workforce further down the scale, or even take it out on clients, which can be fatal. It's a human reaction — if someone humiliates or humbles us we need to do the same ourselves, just to recover from the bruising our ego has taken.

Our current business behaviour is still a throwback to the Eighties. Power was the thing then and it was each person for himself or herself. It was the thing to do well — naked ambition was applauded, greed was an admirable quality. You worked for yourself and yourself alone, clawing your way over the corporate debris to get to the top, no matter how many casualties you produced along the way.

Companies became team-orientated — sectioned off into departments that saw one another as the enemy, rather than seeing themselves as part of one corporate unit. Non-co-operation became the norm, with departments or teams often vying with one another for the same clients.

This was and is bad for business. In a healthy company we should all see ourselves as part of the whole, working in the same direct manner for the same successes. Good etiquette is part of this scenario. It means we treat our colleagues as we would like to be treated ourselves.

Bad manners can often be unintentional — or maybe you think you're too busy to say 'please' and 'thank you' when you have to make a request in the office. Ignorance is no defence, though. We should show respect for fellow workers and treat them with courtesy. You need to keep updated, too. Applying some of the oldfashioned etiquette rules to modern business practice can be every bit as controversial as being deliberately rude.

EXERCISE

*Give your manners a quick MOT by answering the
following questions:*

1. *A junior colleague makes a mistake. Do you bawl
   him or her out:*
   a) *There and then — he or she must be shown on
      the spot, no matter who is listening; or*
   b) *Later, in the privacy of your office.*
   c) *Do you leave a note on his or her desk instead?*

2. *A group of male and female colleagues are sitting in
   a meeting room when a female visitor arrives. Who
   should stand up when she walks in?*
   a) *Nobody.*   b) *All of them.*   c) *The men.*

3. *You have an appointment with a visitor but you're
   delayed. How should you handle it?*
   a) *Turn up when you can, apologising profusely.*
   b) *Pop down to your visitor to apologise for the
      delay and give him or her a realistic estimate of
      how long the wait should be.*
   c) *Call reception and ask them to break the news.*

4. *You want to have a meeting with a colleague. Do you:*
   a) *Call and ask him or her to come to your office.*
   b) *Pop to his or her office and suggest a suitable
      venue.*
   c) *Ask someone who is passing the colleague's office
      if he or she could pass the message on.*

5. *How should you greet and bid farewell to visitors?*
   a) *Greet them with a nod and see them off at the
      door of your office.*
   b) *Come round the desk to offer your hand and take
      them right to the exit (or at least the lift).*
   c) *Wait for them to put their hands out first, get
      your secretary to offer tea and take them back to
      reception.*

6. *How do you refer to your colleagues:*

b) *Women, men — or by name.*

c) *Ladies, gentlemen.*

Answers: *Mostly a's — shame on you!*

                 Mostly b's — your manners are impeccable.

                 Mostly c's — Your etiquette has rust on it.

DRIVEN TO DISTRACTION

Do you annoy your colleagues through plain bad manners? A leading financial company recently did a survey among their staff and came up with the TOP THIRTY PET HATES. See if any of these make you blush.

1. Turning up late for meetings or failing to send apologies.
2. Interrupting others on the phone.
3. Talking loudly with others in front of someone else's desk.
4. Signing onto someone's PC and not signing off again.
5. Borrowing other people's equipment or stationery and not returning it.
6. Jamming the photocopier and leaving it for someone else to repair.
7. Setting the photocopier for multiple copies and leaving it that way.
8. Not holding the lift when others are approaching.
9. Putting the phone down when you've dialled the wrong number instead of apologising.
10. Forgetting to tell your secretary/colleagues your whereabouts.
11. Smoking in corridors or in other people's workspace.
12. Removing chairs from one meeting room to another and not replacing them.
13. Leaving the meeting room in a mess.
14. Shouting at colleagues across the office.
15. Not replying to invitations.
16. Not returning time sheets and other forms on time.
17. Leaving for holiday without clear handover instructions.

18. Never getting drinks for others from the coffee machine.
19. Not returning phone calls.
20. Failing to provide a prompt answer to simple queries.
21. Hijacking meetings by straying from the agenda to discuss your own concerns.
22. Assuming a woman answering the phone is automatically someone's secretary.
23. Unhelpfulness when answering another's call — eg not offering to take a message.
24. Leaving meetings early because you've deliberately double-booked.
25. Abrupt emails with no greeting at the beginning or sign-off at the end.
26. Letters or memos without a personal signature.
27. Eating in lift or corridors.
28. Not introducing people who have never met — even if both are internal.
29. Disappearing for lunch without ensuring the phones are covered.
30. Answering the phone during a meeting and talking for ages while your colleagues wait for you.

(List by courtesy of Coopers & Lybrand)

And here are a few extras:
• Swearing, nattering, non-stop nibbling.
• Grooming yourself at your desk.
• Whistling.
• Knuckle cracking.
• Sounding annoyed or depressed when you answer the phone.
• Refusing to help colleagues.
• Whispering.
• Being sexist or racist.
• Telling dubious jokes.
• Being moody.
• Being patronizing.
• Boasting about hangovers.
• Yawning loudly.
• Asking secretaries to do private chores.

- Expecting priority from a shared secretary.
- Asking other colleagues to lie for you. Etc. etc . . . .

CHARM

A lot of bad-mannered people are also very charming, even though that might sound like a contradiction in terms. Don't be fooled — just because they smile and flutter their eyelashes as they ask you to collect their dry cleaning for them/get them yet another cup of coffee from the machine/ cover for them when they're late, it doesn't make their behaviour o.k.

THE PERFECT COLLEAGUE

A checklist for perfect corporate manners, then:

1. Treat colleagues and clients with respect.
2. Be courteous to all visitors to the company, whether they are clients or somebody trying to sell something.
3. Be punctual and — if you can't — be realistic when estimating the length of delay. 'I'll be with you in a minute' is unproductive if you then take ten minutes or half an hour. Turn up for appointments at other companies at least five minutes early — you never know how long it will take you to get from reception to the office.
4. Greet colleagues positively in the morning.
5. Don't be sexist — there are no men and women in business, there are only people. The old etiquette rules of opening doors and generally treating women as sickly invalids does not apply in business. One company still has a rule that women should be allowed in and out of a lift first. This leads to some very strange shuffling round when people enter and leave in a mixed group!
   Hold doors open if you want to — but not just for certain genders.
6. Don't say NO — offer alternatives. If someone asks you to do something and you're busy, try to negotiate instead of being aggressive.

TELEPHONE TECHNIQUES

Telephones have their own etiquette but people still find it easier to be bolshie to people they can't see.

Like the business letter, the telephone call is a PR exercise for both you and the company you work for. Always practise the following techniques:

1. Keep a pad and pen by the phone, instead of leaving people hanging on while you go off to find one.
2. Use your name and your department when you answer the phone.
3. Sound positive, however busy you are.
4. If you take a message make sure it's a professional one. Take the caller's name, department, company and number. Take a clear message and always repeat it. Write down your own name and the time the message came through.
5. Don't smoke or eat on the phone.
6. Don't have more than one conversation at the same time.
7. Always answer as soon as you pick the phone up — don't leave the caller hanging on while you finish talking to a colleague.
8. Don't hang up without saying goodbye.
9. Listen — don't interrupt.
10. Learn how your phone system works — never use the phrase 'I'll *try* to transfer you', it's sad and unprofessional.
11. If you've got the caller's name and problem pass that on to the other department before you transfer them. That way clients don't keep getting asked 'Can I help you?' as they get transferred around the company.

9 the power of speech

Did you ever hear your voice on tape? Did you like it?

If you did you're in the minority. Most of us hate the sound of our own voices but are too lazy to do anything about it. Like our body language we feel there is little that can be done about it — it's just the way we are.

Of course this is wrong, as well as being defeatist. If you've got something to say, why not make sure the message is heard? A lot of bad speech habits stem from a low sense of self-worth. While we are talking, a small voice in the back of our mind is telling us what we are saying is rubbish. It's not interesting enough. We're not informed enough to be giving this opinion. The listeners are bored. They will disagree with our main proposal and, by golly, they'll be right.

Once this voice gets our attention, the effects are disastrous. We may shut up altogether or we may develop verbal diarrhoea, cramming in as many words as we can to prevent anyone saying anything to contradict us. We may mumble, or we can start to stammer. All this will happen when you start listening too closely to your own words.

IMAGINARY VOICES

Newscasters develop an ability to talk when other messages are buzzing into their ears via a hidden transmitter. We're not newscasters, though. When we hear more than one voice at a time we get confused and clam up. This is what is happening if you listen to your own negative voice while you're trying to talk.

Imagine making a speech while another voice is talking to you, yet — when we get nervous — the conversation goes something like this:

'Ladies and gentlemen . . .'
'You need to clear your throat. You should have sipped some water.'
'It gives me great pleasure to address you here today . . .'
'Did you check your flies?'
'And to talk on a subject closest to my heart . . .'
'What on earth was the subject? What was I going to talk about? Where are my notes?'
'The cause and effects of The Industrial Revolution . . .'
'And I can see from your smug grins that you all know a lot more about it than I do.'

The speech would be a disaster. Yet this is the sort of thing we allow to happen all the time. Of course we should all think before we speak, and a good communicator will judge the reaction of the listener while he or she is speaking. What we need to avoid are the unnecessarily negative messages that fog our brain and handicap our speech patterns.

If you have decided to say something — anything — you should communicate that message as clearly as possible. Here are some tips to help to develop an effective speaking style.

1. POSTURE

If you are slumped or curled up you won't be using your lungs to full capacity, and lungs are the bellows of the voice. Exercise the rib muscles by using the lungs to full capacity.

EXERCISES:

a. Blowing up balloons is a good exercise — try four a day until you can inflate them easily.

b. Another useful exercise is to sit upright in a chair with your fingertips on your abdomen. Exhale all the air from your lungs and then breathe in slowly until the lungs are full and your stomach extended. Try this several times until your lungs have been used to full capacity.

c. Breathe in. Hold the breath and then expel it quickly, in a burst, with a loud shout. You'll feel embarrassed at first but keep doing it until you find your lungs projecting the noise and making it fuller.

d. Find a long passage in a book and read it out loud — loudly — getting as far as you can without taking a breath and without letting your voice drop.

---

2. TONE

A voice that is flat and toneless is boring and a barrier to effective communication. Work on improving the pitch and tone of your own voice. Listen to yourself speaking out loud and see how much tone can add to the emphasis of a statement. Say the following phrase out loud in four different ways:

'Thank you so much for inviting me to your lovely party. I really enjoyed myself.'

Change the pitch and tone so that you sound:

a) Sincere.
b) Sarcastic.
c) Surprised.
d) Angry.

Repeat the exercise, only this time watch your face in a mirror as you 'act' each emotion. See how your expressions change with each one. You'll smile to sound sincere, smirk to sound sarcastic, raise your eyebrows to sound surprised and frown to sound angry. Facial expressions affect the tone of the voice, which is why it's important to remember to smile, even when you're talking on the phone.

Reading out loud is a good way to exercise the pitch and tone of your voice. Do it regularly, sitting alone in a quiet room and reading dramatic passages aloud from a book.

When we get nervous our facial muscles tense up, too, and a set jaw and rigid lips will make the voice more toneless than usual. Limbering-up exercises will help get rid of that rigidity, just as an athlete will warm up his or her muscles before competing in a race.

<u>Jaw</u> — To loosen the jaw, try working your way through each of the consonants, exaggerating each movement of the mouth as you pronounce them. Then try repeating the following phrase doing the same exaggerated expressions:

'Round and round and up and down with ease for she's so angry.'

<u>Lips</u> — To warm up the lips keep repeating the letter 'P' as often as you can, getting louder as you go along. Really

suck the lips in as you begin to pronounce it and 'spit' the letter out, so that your lips purse.

<u>Tongue</u> — Tongue-twisters are the best exercises to make your tongue more flexible. Try any of the old favourites:

'If Peter Piper picked a peck of pickled pepper where's the peck of pickled pepper Peter Piper picked?'

or

'Red leather, yellow leather' repeated several times.

3. PACE

Pace is important. If you rush your words no one will hear them. If you're too slow everyone will be asleep before you're finished. A good investment is a tape recorder. Speak into it and then play it back. Vary the pace of your speech until you think it sounds right and then practise that pace until you can feel it. Always remember that what you have to say is important and worth listening to. If it's worth listening to, then it's worth hearing properly. Take your time.

If you stammer you're probably rushing. Then there is a tendency to rush even faster to make up for lost time. This will only lead to more stammers. When you stammer — stop. People will wait to listen. Then continue at the pace you've been practising.

4. PAUSES

Pauses are useful because they add emphasis to our speech. Yet we can often fear them, thinking the conversation has fallen flat on its face if we allow pauses to happen. Stop being frightened of them. A pause may feel as though it has lasted a few thousand light years, but to the listener it will have been brief.

There is a tendency to jump into conversations whether we hear a pause or not. Always let other people finish what they're saying — and they should extend the same courtesy to you. Interrupt them and expect to get interrupted back.

Some business meetings are run as though a starting pistol has been fired and people have to say as much as they can in the given time. Often this means it's only the loudest and the rudest that get their points across. Overlapping and shouting down conversations are non-productive. Everybody's speaking and nobody's listening.

Keep your own speech to a good pace, vary the tone and pitch and back your points up with eye contact and positive body language, and colleagues should stop and listen to what you have to say.

5. MUMBLING

This is what happens when we don't have faith in our own words. Look up as you speak. If you speak at the floor only the carpet will listen.

6. JARGON

Jargon is the enemy of effective communication. Yet there are whole industries hell-bent on creating newer, longer, stupid-sounding words that nobody outside the business can understand. Creating nonsensical jargon is the worst form of power-posturing. Why not just go ahead and create a whole new language so that you can only be understood by a handful of people?

Jargon is the by-product of profound insecurity. It's clever-clogs stuff, using long, complicated phrases instead of simple short words that have been around for years. The computer industry is probably more riddled with jargon than any other — it's their life-blood. If they're not creating new phrases and words each and every day then there's something wrong, the business is stagnant.

Asking what a new word or phrase means is a bit like being the small boy in Hans Christian Andersen's *The Emperor's New Clothes* — daring to do something that will make you a laughing stock.

Stop using jargon. Delete it from your speech. Employ a jargon box (like a swear box) in your office and donate the thousands you collect to a worthy charity. If it's not stopped, things will get worse and then we'll be calling clocks 'Terrestrial Rotation Emulators', windows 'Passive Solar Illumination Assemblies' and personnel officers 'Human Resources Managers'.

7. WAFFLE

If you work on your pauses, you should eliminate waffle at the same time. Saying anything is *not* better than saying nothing and it's often better to shut up and just nod sagely.

Waffling can also be a sure sign you're lying. Beware the person who phones in sick for work and spends ten minutes describing his or her symptoms and his or her dramatic collapse on the train. The longer and more complicated the story gets the more you can believe it's fairytale time.

Say what you want to say confidently and concisely and people will appreciate your communication. If you've spoken clearly there should be no need for repetition, unless you're doing a more formal presentation, in which case planned repetition can be used to add emphasis.

The biggest test of your waffle-factor is the answerphone. What do you do if faced with one of these things? Hang up? Leave a rambling message and then phone back again with the bits you forgot? Have you ever asked it a question as though it were human? Or can you give a clear and concise message that gets acted upon?

8. ACCENTS

The British are terrible snobs about accents. This makes people worry about theirs until they are shy of communicating effectively. You can never speak like everyone else because we all have different accents. Tone your accent down only to make yourself more easily understood. If listeners think you sound common or stupid it's their problem, not yours.

9. WORDS

Try to keep to positive speech patterns, avoiding dull-sounding terms like: 'I think' or 'possibly' or 'maybe'. If you say something and you believe it, there is no need to tone down or back down, unless you feel you've insulted the other person. We all appreciate positive talk — it's concise and simple and easy to understand. There is no need to fish around for long words just to impress if a shorter one will do.

The other words to avoid are the sort of trendy little make-weights we use to fill the gaps. Words like:

Basically.
You know.
Actually.
Terribly.
Awfully.
In a manner of speaking.
If you like.

or just the annoying and often used 'Um. . .'

Then there are the phrases that grate like nails down a chalkboard:

'I know where you're coming from. . .'
'What you're trying to say is. . .'
'Don't get uptight.'
'Getting down to grassroots.' etc.

10. PUNCTUATION

When we write we use commas and full-stops to give punctuation to our words — when we speak we have to add them verbally. We also have to learn to add emphasis to chosen parts of our talks, so that the listener knows which words are important.

Adding even emphasis to all the words makes whatever we say sound bland and uninteresting, and speech without punctuation drones and bores.

Work on your vocal techniques until you can hear shade and tone in your own speech. Read out loud and listen to how your voice raises or drops on each word. Write out a small speech for yourself and underline all the most important words, then rehearse that talk out loud until you can hear that underlining in your voice.

speak and make people listen

1. Tape your own voice and listen.

2. Practise. Vary pitch and tone. Get used to creating emphasis and be comfortable with pauses.

3. Be concise and to the point. It is better to keep quiet than it is to waffle.

4. Use positive speech, rather than negative and avoid 'trendy' phrases and jargon.

5. Back your words up with eye contact and positive body language.

10 special occasions

During this chapter we're going to be dealing with the specifics because — no matter how hard you work and how much you improve your day-to-day techniques — there will always be those special occasions that will make you want to go crawling back into your warm cosy little shell again.

You know the sort of thing — business presentations, after-dinner speeches, job interviews, big meetings and one-to-one interviews — the sorts of occasions that strike fear in the stoutest of hearts.

We *all* need help with these occasions if we're going to do well. Nobody was born a natural presenter or interviewee — but anyone can learn to improve his or her techniques.

presentations

Public speaking rates high on the Richter Scale of stress. For some reason people would suffer anything rather than the embarrassment of rising to their feet and talking to groups of people. What we don't like we avoid. What we avoid we never get good at.

If we're forced to speak, we gallop through the talk as quickly as possible just to enjoy the relief of getting back to our seats again. Our greatest success comes from having done it and finished — we rarely stop to wonder whether the audience enjoyed it or understood the message.

We watch others talk well and know we could never emulate them — or if we watch someone else make a hash of his or her talk, we just know we're capable of going a whole hash better.

Our head is full of major worries. In our mind the audience becomes the enemy — critical, knowledgeable and terminally intolerant. We have very little to say that is of interest and what we do say will be unintelligible. We don't give ourselves a chance.

Think positive. Compare presentations to a game of chess. Would you start playing without knowing the game and expect to win? Of course not. How do you think the Grand Masters got so good? By practice, of course. Public speaking is a skill and it is a skill that can be learnt. All it needs are the four 'P's' —

PREPARATION
PRACTICE
PERSONALITY
PERFORMANCE

PREPARATION is easy. If we don't bother to prepare it's probably down to cowardice, rather than laziness. Look at the smug smiles on people's faces when they get up and explain that they 'didn't have enough time to prepare'. It's a terrific safety net. What they're telling you is that it's not their fault that their talk is going to be no good. It's out of their hands. They never had a fair chance.

The worst scenario for these people is to give something their best shot and then fail. Then they only have one person to blame — themselves. The thought fills them with horror.

Always do as much preparation as you can for a presentation. Give it your best shot — it's the only way you'll succeed.

Prepare thoroughly and miss nothing. The first thing you'll need to discover may sound obvious but it's something most speakers are ignorant of:

THE POINT

One thing you must be clear about when you prepare is the point of your presentation. If you don't know it your audience will never find out either, because you'll never get to it. Talks without a point are woolly and filled with waffle.

When you're planning your talk you should discover the point of it straightaway. Write it at the top of the page before you begin your notes.

Don't confuse the point with the subject, either.

'Bringing back hanging' is just the subject of a talk. 'Getting people to campaign to bring back hanging' is the point or objective.

ENTHUSIASM

Ask yourself why you're speaking. If the answer comes back: 'Because I was told I had to' then ask again until you come up with a more positive answer. Nobody wants to listen to a speaker who is just talking for the sake of it. To give a good talk you must be enthusiastic about three things:

Your Audience
Your Subject
Your Presentation

Aim your talk in a certain direction. What are your objectives? To fill ten minutes with rambling waffle? Or maybe to educate the listeners? Or entertain them? To sell something to them? Do you want some reaction or action from them at the end?

Many sales presentations have fallen down because the pitch had no real point to it, apart from explaining how good a product was. People listened and then went home. Nobody told them what the next steps were if they wanted to buy.

People like to be told *why* they're listening to a talk. Teaching nurses resuscitation techniques is only valuable if they're told they will be expected to use the techniques to save lives. Schoolchildren always listen better if they're told *why* they are learning something. If we don't know what's expected of us we just listen and forget.

FISHBONES

Fillet your talk like a fish. The point of the talk is the biggest bone of the lot — it's the mainstay that the smaller bones will be attached to. Those smaller bones are all the points that argue your objective. Then add the flesh that is the actual discussion of those points.

If something doesn't aid your main objective, discard it as waffle. It's better to give a talk that is brief and to the point than one that is long and meandering.

If you've prepared your talk and want to shorten it or make it more centred cut it down to five minutes or less, no matter how long it is — you'll soon find out what your major points are — and then you can begin to lengthen it again.

Make sure you are prepared with enough knowledge to fill your performance. A lot of us go in on a knife edge, knowing just about enough about the subject to fill the time but no more. To give a ten minute talk you need two hours of knowledge — that way you won't have a seizure if somebody asks you a question.

THE STRUCTURE

A talk without a strong structure is like a novel without a plot. Most speakers are happy to work out what they're going to say to their audience but many forget their introduction and their ending. Most effective talks, however formal or informal, work on a three-part structure that is simplicity itself — The Beginning, The Middle Bit and The End.

BRAINSTORMING

Get to that structure by starting with a controlled brainstorm. Mark out six columns on a large sheet of paper and throw ideas down into each column as and when they occur to you.

Most people planning a presentation write it like a school essay — starting from the top of the page with the introduction, working through the middle and then to the end. Unfortunately our brains don't work in such a logical way and you may find yourself staring at a blank sheet of paper, trying to work out your opening remarks.

The columns should make up the six stages of your talk

— the first one is for the subject, the second for the point and objectives, the third for any limitations, like time and audience knowledge, the fourth for any points you think your audience might want to make or disagree with, the fifth should be filled with the main meat of your talk and the sixth with the summary — how you're going to finish.

Write any ideas down, no matter how stupid they sound, until you've exhausted all your material. Then and only then begin to tidy the talk up, discarding anything you don't believe will work and moulding the rest into the three-part format — remember? The Beginning, The Middle Bit and The End.

The Beginning

Pause and smile before you start to speak — remember it's important your audience like you and that you show you like them and are pleased to be speaking to them. It doesn't matter if this is a blatant lie — smile sincerely, nevertheless.

Make your introduction sound interesting and make yourself appear confident. Show you know your subject. A few nerves are understandable but ignorance is not. Keenness is contagious — let your audience know you want to speak on your subject and that you find it fascinating.

An easy way of opening is to tell your audience what it is you're going to talk about, and list the objectives or aims of your talk.

Nervous speakers often start by talking themselves down:

'You must excuse me, I'm rather nervous. . .'
'I'm afraid I don't know too much about this subject. . .'
'I'm sorry if this is boring but. . .'

have to be three of the most common dismal openings to any talk. Anyone using these lines deserves to have a black bag lowered over his or her head immediately and be dragged kicking and screaming off the stage.

The introduction might be a good time to recognize any

of your audience's objections, too — to make them feel more at ease. *'I know you're all waiting to eat lunch so I shall keep this talk short and to the point...'* could be the most popular opening ever invented.

'Ladies and gentlemen...' is too formal unless the occasion demands it. If you start too formally it's very difficult to break out of that vein and your whole talk will possibly end up sounding pompous.

Scrub out any long words you can't spell and stick to your own style and manner of delivery.

Only use jokes and humour if you're that type of person naturally. There's nothing worse than listening to someone with a sense of humour bypass trying to deliver pre-scripted jokes during his or her speech. It will make the audience break out in a sweat and ulcers. Be positive — but understand your limitations at the same time.

Don't try to speak without notes — that's called overconfidence and — to be honest — you're asking for trouble. Your notes are your lifeline — you may find you don't have to use them but at least they are there if you do.

Never script yourself, though. If you start reading word-for-word from your notes you'll sound boring and unnatural. Look at your notes. Did you write things like 'Good morning...' and 'My name is...' That was a bad way to start if you want to give a natural-sounding talk.

The best notes are made up of bullet points printed in large print, using different coloured pens to remind you of the structure. Cards can be useful, or you might like to place larger sheets of paper on a nearby table, to keep your hands free altogether. Huge, flapping sheets of A4 will cause trouble and so will titchy writing that you can only see if you peer.

ROOM SERVICE

Prepare your space. Find out all you can in advance about the room where you're going to speak, and move things to your satisfaction.

1. Make sure you have room to move. Don't lock yourself into the small gap between the flip chart and the table, push them back so that there is room to manoeuvre.
2. Check your visual aids and make sure that a) they work and b) they can be seen easily by the entire audience. If there are wires trailing across the floor stick them down before you trip over them. Find out who, if anyone, is speaking before you and make sure they don't need to use anything you've requisitioned, though.
3. Try not to have barriers between yourself and your audience. It might feel comforting to duck behind a desk or a lectern or even a nearby flip chart, but you will lose a lot of the power of your communication if you do.
4. If you have a choice, arrange your audience's seats in a horseshoe-shape. People always like to hide at the back, so have as few rows as possible. Get a colleague to sit in a back seat and check you're audible when you speak.
5. Don't plan to sit while you talk, unless you're speaking to just one person. When you sit down the audience sits mentally, as well, and you take a lot of the impact out of your talk. Perching on a desk is not quite as bad, though check the table first to make sure it's not wobbly.
6. Is there a clock easily visible from where you're standing? If not, take your own table clock because checking your watch constantly looks unprofessional.
7. Find out whether you'll need to dim lights or close blinds when you use slides or overheads. If so, make sure you know how to operate those things.
8. Do you have to use a microphone? If so, sound checks will be necessary.
9. Will there be any distractions in the room while you're talking, eg phones, food being served, people drifting in and out etc.

10. Is the room too hot or too cold?

11. Is there water for you to drink?

GET A GRIP

Take control of your audience, too. Find out as much as you can about them in advance, because the more your talk is tailored to their needs and their knowledge the more successful it will be. Try to work out what they will be expecting and what they will enjoy or learn from. What questions might they ask and what will their objections be? Not everyone will agree with everything you say but you'll handle those objections effectively if you anticipate them.

Handling Difficult Questions

Questions should always be encouraged when possible — it shows the audience are listening and it gives you a chance to deal with any problems that you might never have known about otherwise.

1. Wrestling the Questions The only problem with inviting questions is how to orchestrate them to your best advantage. Most speakers tell their audience in advance that there will be a question session at the end of the talk. This means the presentation won't get interrupted and it gives the audience some time to think about what they might ask. The only disadvantage is that they might not bother. Your talk will end on a low note if you cheerily invite questions, only to be met with resounding silence.

Plan for that kind of disaster and, whatever you do, don't let the silence go on too long. Make a question up yourself if you have to. Pretend someone asked something over coffee — anything rather than stand there with egg on your face. Often once the ball is rolling the questions will start coming in thick and fast — it's just a case of getting over that first hurdle.

Another ploy is to invite questions as you go along, or at the end of each segment of your talk. Inviting a free-for-all requires confidence on your behalf, though, as you may find you quickly lose control of your presentation. Also your structure may suffer if delegates keeping veering off the main point. Allowing time at the end of each segment may be a safer technique.

2. <u>Listening</u> Always show you're listening to any questions that are asked. Use the listening techniques discussed under the body language section of this book and let the questioner speak without interruption. Repeat the question to the audience in case they didn't hear all of it.

3. <u>Fair Shares</u> If several people have questions always allow each person one only (if you have time) before returning to anyone with a second question. People don't like queue-jumpers.

4. <u>Greedy</u> If someone is hogging the question time, or asking questions that stray off the point, ask if anyone else has an interest in that particular aspect and, if not, tell the questioner that you'll deal with the point later, when the talk is over. Never allow anyone to hijack your talk.

5. <u>Stumped</u> We all get questions we don't know the answer to from time to time. Either throw the question out to the rest of the room or tell the questioner you don't know but will find out. It can help to use flattery: 'That's a very good question. . . .' etc.

6. <u>Hostile</u> Never, ever, lose your temper in the face of a hostile questioner. Don't even show you're annoyed — not even the slightest clenching of the teeth. Keep in control at all times. Sarcasm, rudeness or ridicule will only alienate the rest of your audience. Be professional. If you're prey to a hostile questioner ask for his or her name and company before the question is asked. This often takes the wind out of his or her sails.

7. Cut Off Learn how to cut people off if you have to. Thank them for their questions but remind them of the time remaining. If necessary, warn them they'll miss lunch/ refreshments if you don't get on. Use eye contact and assertive body language to back your statement up.

PRACTICE

Once you've prepared your presentation start practising it and don't stop until you're bored to tears. Boredom is good — it means you're not terrified any more, though apprehension is good too — when you lose the fear you become blasé and lose the 'edge' of your performance.

Start with a tape recorder and work up to humans. (You can bypass the family dog this time — he's suffered enough with the effects of your eye contact.)

Find people who are willing to listen without giggling and who will give you a critical review at the end. Rehearsal helps you to feel more confident and it helps to time the talk, too. Ask your listeners to be candid about the following questions:

1. Was the point of the presentation obvious and well-made?
2. Was there any waffle, or did you keep to the point?
3. What did they understand to be the most important parts of the talk?
4. Were these messages clear and underlined?
5. Did any visual aids help or hinder the message?
6. Which parts were dull or boring?
7. Was the introduction interesting and positive? Did it make them want to listen?
8. Did you remember to smile?
9. Did you use eye contact?
10. Were there any annoying gestures or body language?
11. Could they hear everything that was said?
12. Was the tone of voice varied and interesting or too monotonous?
13. Was the summary clear and confident?
14. Did you say 'um' too much?

PERSONALITY

If we don't like the messenger we don't like the message. It's as simple as that. If we see the worst we expect the worst. Look positive. Get up to talk with an expression of enthusiasm — for your message as well as your audience. Pause and smile at them before you begin, don't stand there with the haunted expression of someone who is gazing down into the bowels of hell.

Remember your body language. Move if you like but move in time with your speech, letting your gestures add emphasis to your message. Empty your pockets before you get up and get rid of anything you might find yourself fiddling with.

Stand in a central position and avoid any defensive gestures, like crossing your arms, rocking from foot to foot, backing away and looking down.

Space your feet comfortably and make sure the weight is

evenly balanced. Let your arms relax and don't tuck the elbows into the waist. Stand straight but not too erect and keep eye contact with your audience — *all* your audience. Some people find themselves looking at just one person or one side of the room. Sweep the entire group.

Don't stuff your hands in your pockets but don't let your arms flap around, either. You're trying to look relaxed and natural, which is the exact opposite of the way you feel. Try it all the same, though.

If someone asks a question stand your ground, or even lean slightly towards them to show how pleased you are to be given an opportunity to air even more of your knowledge.

An important point to remember is that a good speaker will always be aware of the needs of the audience. A good talk is one that caters for those individual needs — not one that is so rigidly pre-rehearsed that there is no altering it or going back once it is started.

Different audiences react in different ways. Some will be quiet, others quickly bored and some totally fascinated and absorbed by everything you have to say. The same delivery wouldn't be appropriate to every group. Skilled speakers will read reactions from the audience and think on their feet to vary the content or style of delivery.

Imagine you began your talk with a joke and nobody laughed. Would you press on regardless with the other twenty gags you'd planned or would you make a mental note to skip them as the audience obviously had little sense of humour?

What if you've planned a thirty-minute speech and you can see the audience getting restless after the first few minutes — would you go on in the same tone, using the same delivery?

If you can read your audience while you're talking you will find it easier to second-guess their needs. Watch for symptoms of boredom or disagreement. See if they're changing position restlessly or looking at their watches frequently. People send visual signals when they want to join in. Often you can spot people who have something to say and invite them to speak before they've interrupted you. They may become more upright or begin to raise their hands. Perhaps their expressions look puzzled or they start to frown, to show they wish to question you.

If they're all yawning, either open a window or make your talk more active, or both. Introduce a visual aid or invite feedback to keep them awake a little longer. If you sense silent disapproval, invite questions at that point so that you can deal with their queries, rather than letting them fester.

And never try to compete with food, drink or ringing phones. If they can hear or see lunch being served or they know you're running over time when they should be eating, their only thought will be for the food. If coffee has arrived while you're talking, they'll miss the rest of the talk because they'll be worrying it's getting cold — and a ringing phone is the ultimate distraction. Get it dealt with, rather than talking through it.

PERFORMANCE

This may sound like a grand term if you're just addressing a handful of colleagues — but once you rise to your feet you owe it to anyone fortunate enough to be listening to make your performance as professional as possible.

Professional doesn't have to mean slick — but it should mean effective communication without the distractions caused by flapping about and showing upside-down slides.

We all have short concentration spans, too. To communicate effectively you should make your presentation as interesting as possible.

Any talk will sag after the opening minutes, and the longer it goes on the more likely the audience are to switch off. A talking head is dull unless the delivery is magnificent. Someone moving and using visual aids for illustration is a lot less likely to hear snoring while he or she is talking.

VISUAL AIDS

So-called visual aids can be a help or a hindrance, depending on how you use them. Before you think about employing any of them, though, always examine your motives — are you using it to help *you* or your *audience*? They should not be used as a crutch. If you think the flip chart looks like something handy to hide behind, or the slides are great because they mean the audience won't be looking at you, then you're using extremely faulty logic. If you believe the overhead will help to underline your major points and make the delegates remember them better, you're well on the way to a great presentation.

FLIP CHART

Can be pre-planned, with well-printed headings, points or even sketches, or can be used to throw down major points or feedback as you go along. Always check spelling and make sure your handwriting is legible.

Good Points: Can make a talk more dynamic and interesting and will emphasize the bullet points.

Can also help with the structure if you list these points up there beforehand.

Drawbacks: Easy to trip over or duck behind.
Bad spelling will make you appear illiterate.
Pens can be fiddled with.

Planning: Make sure there is enough paper.
See if you're tall enough to flip the used pages back, or strong enough to tear the perforated ones off.
Practise writing without turning your back to the audience — it makes them bored and fidgety.
Check the pens aren't dried up.

OVERHEAD

Good Points: As per flip chart.

Bad Points: The monster from hell if used badly. Older models look huge and ugly and may hum or even vibrate.
Seeing the pre-planned acetates may lead to reading

verbatim, which will sound like the worst kind of scripting.

These things bring out the worst in presenters. One of the most blush-making techniques is the 'peek-a-boo' method, where speakers have a list of ten major points on one acetate and go through them one at a time, hiding the others from view with a sheet of paper. At some point the paper always slips too far, revealing a new point too early.

<u>Planning:</u> Don't be mean — if you have ten things to say list them on ten separate acetates and put them up one at a time. Use the eleventh to list all the points as a summary at the end.

Always switch the machine off in between points as delegates will prefer to look at an empty lit screen rather than at you.

Avoid turning your back to look at the screen and don't talk to it, either.

Don't be too wordy on your acetates and never read them word-for-word to the audience.

Try not to stand over the machine while it's switched on. Uplighting is notoriously unflattering, being traditionally used to great effect in most of the Frankenstein movies.

SLIDES

<u>Good Points:</u> Pictures do paint a thousand words.

It can be used for a large audience, if necessary.

<u>Bad Points:</u> The snooze-factor when the lights have to go down.

The fact that slide projectors can be moody little fellers to deal with.

The curse of the upside-down slides.

<u>Planning:</u> Get your machine into position and run through your slides before you start.

Use a remote control if there is one, or back-projection, which is even better.

Try to dim the lights, rather than extinguish them altogether, as you should still be visible and the delegates should be able to take notes.

Use the projector for pictures, rather than words.

Tape down trailing wires for obvious reasons.

SAMPLES, PHOTOS OR OBJECTS FOR SCRUTINY

Good Points: Few. Only use if there is no alternative.

Bad Points: Legion. Distraction is the main one. Never pass anything around your audience if you can help it. One will be looking at it while all the others will be looking at them. The ones nearby will be waiting for their look and the ones furthest away will be impatient, thinking the subject will have changed before they get their go.

Put them on a table nearby and the audience's eyes will remain enigmatically glued on them.

VIDEO

Good Points: Good videos can be interesting for the audience and effective illustrations if used as a training tool.

Bad Points: The same snooze-factor as the lights go off and the delegates prepare to engage in a bit of telly-watching.

Some of the professional training videos use top actors and comedians. If you're speaking next you may find them a hard act to follow.

Planning: Make sure you're well-acquainted with the contents of the video so that you don't find to your horror that it contradicts points you've made beforehand.

Try to use them directly before lunch, if possible.

DRESSING UP

Wear clothes that look smart and feel comfortable for a presentation. Make sure there is a lot of movement in whatever you're wearing and that you won't be handicapped by sleeves you can't reach out in, shoes that make you feel awkward, ties that go crooked as soon as you clear your throat, or skirts that ride up when you sit down or walk.

Don't wear clothes that are too fussy — or that distract from you and the message you're giving.

Try not to look too boring, either — if your clothes look stuffy and out-of-date the audience will think your viewpoint is, too.

Empty your pockets and avoid wearing any jewellery or accessories you might fiddle with.

Don't start dressing or grooming yourself once you're on your feet. Jackets shouldn't be done up or undone while you're talking, you shouldn't be picking hairs or dust off your jacket and you should never fiddle with your hair, either.

It's a bigger mistake to be too casual or scruffy for your audience than to be too smart. If in doubt always veer on the side of formality. At least the audience will be flattered you made the effort.

golden rules for positive presenting:

1. Always keep your audience in mind and tailor your talk to them and their needs.
2. Be yourself — don't try to use different accents or unfamiliar long words or terms — speak in your own style and use your own strengths, rather than copying others.
3. Know the point of your presentation.
4. Be knowledgeable about your subject — always know too much rather than too little.
5. Don't be boring. Boredom has to be the biggest block to effective communication. If *you're* bored, they will be, too.
6. Prepare your presentation well in advance.

7. Use brainstorming to write down your ideas, then tidy into a three-part structure.
8. Rehearse and invite feedback.
9. Know the room you'll be speaking in.
10. Dress comfortably and appropriately.
11. Don't have a drink first.

interview blues

'In an interview, you as the interviewee should focus the discussion on yourself. As an interviewer, I am interested in your talents, your achievements and your personality, not that of any other parties.' — Jacqueline Moyse, Director of Training. InterContinental Hotels.

Approaching an interview is a lot like preparing for a sales presentation, except this time the product you'll be selling is yourself.

Just as with the presentation, never go into an interview without thorough preparation, as chancing your luck rarely pays off.

PREPARATION
1. Find out as much as you can about the company and the job beforehand.
2. List your own skills and good points on paper. Study them. These are your major selling points.
3. Always plan the journey and allow for unforeseen problems. Better to have time for a coffee and a think than to run in late.
4. Imagine you're the one doing the interviewing. Why *should* you be given the job?
5. Pick your outfit carefully — never choose something you haven't worn before. Pull a chair up in front of a full-length mirror and sit down in it. Does your chosen outfit sit well too? Do you feel comfortable? Can you move and gesticulate freely? If not, pick something else. A business suit is usually acceptable for any interview

— remember an interview is a formal occasion and most interviewers are more impressed by someone who has made an effort with his or her appearance than someone who looks untidy or too casual.

6. Make sure the outfit is clean and ironed and in good repair. Keep in mind the type of job and company you're applying to and make sure your outfit is suitable. Check your shoes are clean and immaculate. Don't look too dressy and avoid looking as though you're in your Sunday best. You should look comfortable in smart clothes, not as though they're just something you dug out for the occasion.

7. Use visualization techniques to see yourself doing well at the interview.

8. Carry an appropriate bag. Something businesslike is best — nothing crammed full to overflowing and no plastic bags. Bad weather often means the need for overcoats, boots and wet umbrellas. Take two plastic bags inside your own bag, one for the folded umbrella once you're inside and one for your boots once you've changed into the smart shoes you've taken with you. Plan things like this carefully so that you don't walk in looking like a mess.

9. Make sure your etiquette is o.k. Don't offer your hand first for the handshake, do wait to be offered a seat before you sit down, etc.

10. Don't accept the offer of tea if you're really nervous as bone china has a loud rattle and it's difficult to drink when you're trying to speak.

overall

Always sit into the back of a chair, rather than perching on the edge. Get in front of a mirror and practise the manoeuvre. What will you do with your arms? Crossing them will make you look guarded. If you have arms to your chair you can rest your elbows on them and let your hands hang loosely in your lap.

Keep your back straight and your shoulders relaxed, rather than hunched. Hold your head up in a natural-looking way when you talk, otherwise you may find you're mumbling into your chest.

Always put bags down on the floor — never sit clutching them on your lap.

Probably the worst seats to deal with are the casual, low-slung settees they have in some interview rooms. The idea is to put the interviewee at his or her ease but it's difficult to lounge in a smart business suit.

If you're interviewed by one person your eye contact should be simple, but panel interviews can be more difficult. Always begin your answer by looking at the person who asked it — but then direct it at the entire panel. Try to use the same sort of even dispersal of eye contact that you would use during a presentation. Try not to avoid looking at the interviewer with the dour expression in favour of the one with the welcoming smile.

Plan your answers to questions you're likely to be asked and, like a presentation, don't be afraid of pauses. It can be too easy to give a good answer the first time and then nervously fill the following pause with all the wrong things.

Think of all those awkward questions that crop up with alarming regularity, like:

'Why did you leave your last job?'
'Where do you see yourself in five years' time?'
'Tell me about yourself!'
'How would your worst enemy describe your faults?'
'What are your priorities in life?'
'What do you think you have to offer this company?'
'Any questions?'

meetings

Busy executives attending meetings or presentations must know:

'Why am I here?'
'What is expected of me?'
'What's in it for me?'

This having been established, the productivity of the meeting will be greatly enhanced.' — Director of Training. InterContinental Hotels.

Generally speaking, meetings should be planned like a presentation — you should be aware of the point of the meeting and plan your own contribution. You must avoid waffle or time-consuming deviations from the main point and you should consider the best way to make your contribution effective and your communications successful.

BUTTING IN

The biggest problem for the individual at a meeting is not being able to get a word in edgeways. Maybe you have valuable contributions to make but perhaps the meeting is being hijacked by the more assertive members of the group.

If you're not the chair of the meeting, it may be difficult to take control. By the time there is a sufficient gap for you to jump in you'll often find yourself airing your grievance at not being listened to, rather than using valuable time to make your point. Approach any meetings assertively and confidently with your points clear in your head but — like a presentation or an interview — be prepared to listen, too.

1. **Be positive.**
   If you have a point to make, make it a positive one. Whingers very rarely hold the attention. If you have a disagreement to voice try to phrase it in a positive way, so that you don't sound as though you're arguing for the sake of it.
2. **Get to the point.**
   Avoid all the time-consuming chit-chat that can ruin a

business meeting. When you speak, be concise and don't waffle. Plan what you have to say and how you will say it. Talking to a group can be different from talking one-to-one because you will often get less response while you're talking. This often puts people off and makes them nervous because they feel they have 'the floor'. Use assertive body language — eye contact, open gestures etc., and say your piece confidently, without backing down.

Never open with an apology — sound as though you think you have an important contribution to make, too.

3. **Use Body Language.**

   Watch others make their points. People will often announce the fact that they're going to speak visually. Nobody who sits still, staring at his or her hands, will even get a word in edgeways. Lean forward in your seat and place your hands on the table to announce your contribution and give them time to pause and listen. Removing glasses can be a good way of getting attention and so can taking off earrings and placing them on the table. You could raise your hands, palm-up, to get attention or you could raise a finger. Watch others who get their turn to speak easily and see what techniques they use. Shouting may work short-term but it often leads to resentment and nobody wants a meeting where everyone is shouting everyone else down.

4. **Visualizations**

   Like presentations and interviews, build up your confidence prior to a meeting by using the visualization techniques. See yourself speaking up and making your point with confidence. Study the techniques you're using and how you're getting your point across. Plan in the same way as you would with a presentation, working out any objections the others may have to your viewpoint and working out how to deal with them effectively.

11 asserting yourself

Being assertive doesn't mean getting your own way at all times, nor is it a permanent, fixed style of behaviour. It is an *alternative* method of behaviour — a way of approaching situations so that there are no losers. It's learning how to ask for what you want in a positive manner. It's an increased range of options for dealing with others in a variety of situations — learning how to respond, rather than react.

Like most of the other skills in this book, it's all about taking control.

We relinquish control of our own emotions all too easily, allowing other people to make us upset or make us lose our temper or even make us happy. It's only in extreme circumstances that anyone can force us to feel an emotion, though. All that happens is that a person behaves in a certain way — it's up to us how we choose to react to that behaviour.

A manager could carpet three of her staff. One of them could go away from the carpeting positive and determined to do better, another could be angry and plotting revenge for the slight, and the third could spend the rest of the day in the loo, in floods of tears of self-pity. Each one chose his or her own reaction to the manager's words and each one reacted in a different way.

Of course there could be other factors affecting our reactions, like illness or depression. Maybe you react badly because you're tired or because something else has left you with a feeling of low self-esteem.

The emotional baggage we carry around with us makes it difficult to focus our thoughts on the situation at hand. We live in the past and the future — but all too rarely in the present. When we fly off the handle at a minor upset we're dragging in ghosts of past grievances, rather than dealing with the minor problem in front of us.

We need to learn to focus our thoughts and deal with each situation as it occurs. If we bring less emotional baggage into a dispute we'll come to a satisfactory conclusion quickly and more easily. Scoring points and putting people in their place is not part of the assertiveness style. Trying to understand the other person's point of view while voicing our own thoughts is.

FIGHT OR FLIGHT

Children have two ways of reacting to a problem — they stand their ground and fight it or they run away or cry. As we grow older and our intellect and vocabulary skills increase we have another option open to us — the assertive approach. We learn how to discuss and negotiate. We should also learn that this is often the most effective way of dealing with things, but in fact we don't. We still enjoy the shortcuts of anger or silent acceptance, and we blind ourselves to their long-term defects. Let's face it, there is a lot to be said for blowing your top or playing the long-suffering martyr:

Aggression — The Advantages
1. May make you feel better for getting it off your chest.
2. Will ensure you get your own way.
3. You'll feel great because you didn't back down.
4. You'll think you earned the respect of your colleagues.
5. People won't walk over you.

Passivity — The Advantages
1. You'll have avoided a confrontation.
2. People will still like you.
3. You won't have made yourself unpopular.
4. You avoided any risk.

Great!

However — long-term a lot of those advantages turn sour:

Aggression — Disadvantages

1.　You anger other people.
2.　They return aggression with either aggression or passivity.
3.　They do what you want but with resentment.
4.　It's a difficult pose to maintain without increasing your stress-levels.

Passivity — The Disadvantages

1.　You don't get what you want.
2.　People take you for granted.
3.　You lose self-respect.

With *assertive* behaviour you keep the respect of others naturally, without threatening behaviour. Passivity often leads to lies — if we don't want to do something we often lie our way out of it, just to avoid saying no. You may be asked to babysit, for example, and make up a story about working late, rather than admit you don't want to do it. Lies can lead to other lies, though — which in turn will lead to stress.

You won't always get what you want through being assertive, but at least you'll know you gave it your best shot.

FEAR

Being assertive can be frightening. We're scared of people's reactions if we tell them what we think. The thing to remember, though, is that it is a skill to be used only when it's appropriate, and that neither side should feel humiliated or lowered by the transaction.

If you need to criticize someone or something that criticism should always be relevant. When you refuse a request you should do so in a way that leaves the path for further negotiation open. Always show an understanding of the other person's side of things and treat him or her in a way that you would want to be treated yourself.

SITUATIONS

Imagine you're at work. You have a load of high-priority jobs to do but someone has just given you more work and insisted it be done that morning. What would your reaction be?

Passive:
'o.k., I'll try to do it.'

A short-term sop. Either you do his or her job and annoy all the other people who had asked you first, or you don't do it when you say you will, which will annoy the first person. Maybe you'll quietly do it in your lunch hour, which will annoy you and you'll hate yourself for being such a wimp.

Aggressive:
'Look — you can see how busy I am already. You're always dumping this sort of stuff on me at the last minute — how many pairs of hands do you think I have? Ask someone else to do it!'

Well, you felt great after that, didn't you? But how did the other person feel? Maybe he or she *didn't* know how busy you were. Perhaps he or she will return anger with anger and the whole thing will escalate. What about the atmosphere that's left behind?

Assertive:
'Look — I know how important this work is to you and I'm sure you don't mean to make my job difficult but I've already got a backlog of urgent jobs pending. I can't finish it this morning. Four o'clock would be the earliest.'

There is no need for the other person to feel humiliated and you've put a realistic deadline on the job. You've stated your position honestly without lowering the other person.

Now imagine you've ordered some goods by post and the wrong things have arrived two days late. What would be the appropriate behaviour?

Passive:
Keep the goods and decide never to use the company again, using every chance to moan about the firm to all your friends.

Aggressive:
Phone up to complain: *'Look, are you all stupid there, or what? First I had to wait days for the stuff to arrive, which meant time off work and now I've had to use petrol*

to drive down to the Post Office and pick it up and when I
do I find you've delivered the wrong goods! What the hell
do you think you're playing at?'

Assertive:
'I understand it's Christmas and that your department
must be busy but first I was inconvenienced by the late
delivery and then I discovered they were the wrong goods.
I'm sure this is an oversight but I'd like the goods collected
and a full refund, please.'

Of course, some people will argue with you, no matter
how assertive you're being. When this happens it's
important for you to know what's negotiable and what
isn't. If you stand out for something and then back down
under pressure, you'll find people will always argue in
future because they'll assume you can be battered into
submission every time.

If your position is not negotiable go for the 'broken
record' technique, repeating your point over and over again
instead of arguing.

Imagine someone has asked to borrow some money from
you.

Passive Reaction:
Pay up and whinge later, or:

'I'm sorry, I don't have any cash on me.' (A lie.)
'I thought you went to the cashpoint at lunchtime.'
'I did, but I need that money to buy something tomorrow.'
(Another lie.)
'That's o.k. — I'll get it back to you by then.'
'Sorry — what I meant was I promised to lend it to Roger
today. He's got to order some flowers for his wife's
birthday.'
'That's o.k., then — he can order the flowers on my credit
card and I can borrow the cash from you instead.'

Assertive Reaction:
'I'm sorry, I'm afraid the answer has to be no.'
'I can have it back to you by tomorrow.'

'No — I'm sorry.'
'Until tonight, then.'
'No.'

By restating your decision over and over again you leave no scope for negotiation or argument.

EXERCISE

Practise your own assertive techniques. Write down the Passive, Aggressive and then Assertive responses to each of these three situations:

1. *You have been giving a colleague a lift to work for the past two months and so far he or she hasn't offered to pay towards the petrol. You like the company but you feel the situation is unfair.*

   PASSIVE REACTION:
   AGGRESSIVE REACTION:
   ASSERTIVE REACTION:

2. *You're at a job interview and are asked a sexist question.*

   PASSIVE REACTION:
   AGGRESSIVE REACTION:
   ASSERTIVE REACTION:

3. *You've just had a take-away delivered and are sitting down to relax in front of a video when the phone rings. Your next door neighbour's husband has been taken sick at work and she wants you to babysit while she goes to collect him.*

   PASSIVE REACTION:
   AGGRESSIVE REACTION:
   ASSERTIVE REACTION:

   Read through all your replies out loud. How did they sound? Do you think you could use the assertive

> *ones in reality? Assertive behaviour isn't easy at first and it does take practice. Do remember to make sure it's appropriate, though, before you use it. Some times we would be kinder being passive. Situation number three would probably be one of those times.*

BACKUP

Assertive behaviour will be ineffective if it's not backed up by assertive body language. You may choose assertive words but if someone sees passive body language accompanying them or even hears a whining tone of voice, he or she will tend to react to the tone, or to the body language.

If you're sure of your position then state it with confidence, using upright posture, open gestures and positive eye contact to reinforce the message.

Make sure your vocal skills are well-rehearsed, too. Say what you think in an audible, well-paced way with plenty of pitch and tone to underline the importance of the message.

The danger-zone is straight after you've said your bit — because this is when we're most likely to back down, while we're waiting for the other person's reaction.

Keep your posture and don't look away or down. Don't giggle nervously or smile if it's not appropriate. Avoid any hand-wringing or any dismissive flapping movements that will imply you weren't as serious as you sounded. Also avoid crossing your arms or any nervous gestures, like nail-biting or neck-rubbing. That way the importance and honesty of your message will have been reinforced.

Aggressive Symptoms:
* Shouting
* Frowning
* Pointing
* Shaking your fist
* Slamming doors
* Being sarcastic
* Smirking

- Interrupting
- Swearing
- Glaring
- Staring
- Putting people down
- Passing the buck

Using words like: Stupid, Nonsense, Ridiculous, Idiotic and phrases like: 'So what you're *trying* to say is. . .' and 'What you *ought* to be doing is. . .'

Passive Symptoms:
- Agreeing to do things you don't want to do
- Mumbling or talking quietly
- Apologising a lot
- Waffling
- Crying
- Smiling all the time
- Whingeing about people behind their backs
- Fiddling
- No eye contact

Passive-Aggressive Symptoms:
(By far the most horrendous types to know.)

Quiet in a lecture or meeting but complaining loudly afterwards.

Will smile and agree to things but will plot revenge long-term.

Helpful and friendly but then suddenly, often after long periods of time, will voice resentment at all that help in an over-the-top aggressive way.

Will insist on lending money, buying expensive gifts, helping in some way, but will then make constant reminders of the favour and even feel it gives them a hold over the person they helped.

Will suffer in silence at the time but make sure you're aware of that suffering when it is too late to do anything but feel guilty, eg spend hours sympathising and commiserating when your cat dies and only let you know six months later that his or her father died on the same day. Your guilt will be insurmountable and his or her glee at having put you in such a terrible position will be limitless.

Or such a person will sit bravely through a justified telling-off from the boss then make sure a colleague informs him or her later that he or she had spent the weekend secretly booked into hospital having an appendix/womb/gall bladder removed.

Assertive Symptoms:
Open gestures and relaxed but upright posture.
Confident eye contact without staring.
Ability to make decisions.
Will tell people what they think or want, but only when it's appropriate.
Will always consider the other person's feelings and listen to his or her viewpoint.
Audible, well-paced speech patterns.

twelve great reasons for being more assertive

1. It'll give you more self confidence
2. Greater self-respect, knowing you're in control of your life.
3. Less reliance on others.
4. Less time wasted skirting around problems and confrontations.
5. Less stress.
6. Better atmosphere at work.
7. No build-up of emotions like resentment and anger.
8. You'll be taken for granted less.
9. You'll feel happier.
10. You'll try more because you won't fear rejection or making a mistake.
11. Better career prospects.
12. Being focused on the present makes your work more effective.

conclusion

Reading a book will not improve your image. What it can do is send you riding off into the sunset with an expression of hope on your face. Unlike films, though, the words 'THE END' don't appear at this point, but rather 'THE BEGINNING'. This is the start of your new image — the hard work is up to you. Buying a self-improvement book is to your lifestyle what buying a tracksuit is to losing weight — it will only work if you're prepared to put in the effort.

Now is the time to start planning that effort — right now, while you're still in a positive frame of mind. Set goals and plan deadlines. Don't be modest about your goals but think of them as achievable, not as dreams. Plan a calendar of daily achievements, no matter how small they are, so that the movement is upward, rather than downward or stagnant.

action points

These should be pleasurable and consistent. Some of them may even make you laugh, like installing a 'moan box' on your desk, with every moaner putting money in for charity. List your action points from each chapter of the book and think of each one of them as a step on a ladder.

Some may sound like chores, like pressing clothes each night for the next day, but they'll quickly disappear into the new routine of your life. Feel positive about the changes you'll be making and be open-minded about the results of those changes.

The important thing is to remember to work on the internal as well as the external image. Feel good about yourself as well as enjoying the way you look. Know your strengths and be confident about your abilities. Don't let fear of failure prevent you from trying in the first place and — last of all — stop blaming others and take control of your own life and destiny.